AF207480

Early Carpets and Tapestries on the Eastern Silk Road

Early Carpets and Tapestries on the Eastern Silk Road

Gloria Gonick

ACC ART BOOKS

Contents

FOREWORD

I first met Gloria Gonick in the early 1980s, when she picked me up from the Los Angeles airport, took me to lunch at Marina del Rey, and we spent an afternoon looking at her extensive collections of Asian textiles. From that moment I have admired her keen eye, her insight into the technical complexities of Chinese and Japanese fabrics, and her enquiring mind that tries to make sense of historic textiles. Since that first meeting I have also been lucky to witness her transition from knowledgeable collector to Master's candidate to scholar and curator with what can only be described as an obsession for the fabrics used to decorate Gion Matsuri cart/floats.

Her master's thesis from UCLA, which evolved into her book *Matsuri! Japanese Festival Arts* (UCLA/Fowler Museum of Cultural History Textiles Series 6, 2004), focused on the textiles used at a variety of Japanese festivals (*matsuri*). It included a chapter on textiles imported from abroad. With the aid of several grants Gloria was able to make an in-depth study of the foreign textiles used to decorate festival carts for Kyoto's midsummer Gion Matsuri. While the glamorous luxury textiles from China, India, the Middle East and even Europe have received significant scholarly attention, the wool textiles, which are the focus of this book (thirty-six ink-painted wool tapestries and twenty-one wool-pile carpets), remained largely unknown and only speculatively documented.

The Gion Festival Floats Associations' catalogue perfunctorily identified the ink-painted tapestries as Korean and the wool-pile carpets as regional Chinese. Yet, as Gloria examined these pieces in detail, felt their weight and compared the materials, colours and structures, those identifications just didn't make sense. Gloria embarked on a quest to answer the questions of where these textiles were from, who made them, and how they ended up in Japan. This mission has taken her to back to Japan several times and resulted in over a dozen trips to China, including the most distant parts of northwest China, as well as visits to museum collections around the world.

Gloria has succeeded in tracing the source of these enigmatic textiles despite obstacles, which she categorises as time (five centuries have passed since many of the pieces were acquired), space (the vastness of China) and change (place names, governments, populations, religious practices). She has synthesised data from diverse sources, including structural and technical analysis of the textiles themselves, radiocarbon date testing, an inventory of iconographic motifs, archaeological and architectural evidence in Central Asia and northwest China, historical documents, extensive interviews with regional specialists and oral histories from contemporary descendants of traditional weavers. As a result she now presents convincing arguments as to why the Gion Festival Foundations' two groups of wool textiles are associated with Uyghur weavers.

Specifically she identifies those Uyghurs who left their original homeland in Mongolia in the eighth century to settle in the Ganzhou region of Gansu province. These Turkic-speaking people brought their Manichaean faith, eventually travelling eastward along the Hexi Corridor to establish a number of Manichaean communities along the Yellow River. The sheep from this region supplied Uyghur weavers with the long-staple wool that characterises the textiles used in the Gion Festival. Tapestry weaving and knotted-pile carpet-making are techniques that have a long association with Uyghurs. As Gloria discovered, in their historical contexts the Manichaean elite and their high priests wore the tapestry-woven pieces as ceremonial mantles; high lamas, known as 'Living Buddhas', sat on the pile carpets during audiences.

The xenophobic policies of the Chinese Ming dynasty banned Manichaeism. While formal Manichaean religious practice largely died out during the fifteenth to seventeenth centuries, an overlay of Tibetan Buddhism and Daoism had tended to shield older cultural beliefs until the present day. Contemporary Chinese prejudice tends to lump all Uyghurs with the Islamic groups in Xinjiang that agitate for independence. While perhaps less politically motivated, few scholars have attempted to study the relics recovered from Dunhuang and Central Asian sites from the 1890s to 1930s (artefacts now in London, New Delhi, Paris and St. Petersburg) in the context of the various cultures that continued to inhabit the region. Thus, perhaps inadvertently, they are reinforcing the notion that Manichaeism represents a long-dead culture. In contrast, Gonick's book is a revelation of the persistence of culture in the artefacts it produces.

The book is a celebration of material culture, based on a personal and profound appreciation of objects. Many of the great textile historians of this and the previous generation were able to tease out the complex stories that lie behind, inside and are completely embodied in the textiles they studied, adding significantly to the study of culture, both contemporary and historical. Accordingly, Gloria Gonick's work joins that of Donald King and Dorothy Burnham, Elizabeth Barber and Elena Phipps, whose exploration of discrete and seemingly orphaned clusters of misidentified objects reveals amazing new knowledge.

Gloria likens the imperative of cultures leaving artefacts to human footprints. Both reveal determination and a link to conscious action. Both are evidence of a journey. In *Early Carpets and Tapestries on the Eastern Silk Road*, Gloria takes her readers on a journey of discovery through the historical culture that produced these wool textiles, to the cultures that traded them across vast reaches of Asia, and their continuing journey as ornaments to astonish the gods at an annual festival 4,000 miles and at least 500 years distant from their origin.

John E. Vollmer, New York City 2015

INTRODUCTION

As the Yuan Dynasty (1260–1368 CE) was coming to a close in China, having been violently deposed by the armies of the Ming (1368–1644 CE), important events were taking place across the sea in Japan. These developments would preserve the legacy of the Manichaeans,[1] a frequently proscribed religious minority in China.[2] Manichaean relics preserved in northwest China and in Japan – the art and artefacts of what was once a popular faith in Europe, Asia and Africa, now usually described as 'long extinct' – are the subject of this book.

In 1994 I received a Japan Foundation grant to document in English the fabled foreign textile collections of Kyoto, owned by the city's long-standing Gion Festival Floats Associations (Gion Matsuri Yamaboko Rengokai, hereafter 'the Associations'). By that time I had been studying East Asian textiles and culture for some years. I reviewed the collections extensively in the summer of 1994, returning to Kyoto in 1995 and 1999.[3] Images were made available to me, along with a recently published catalogue of the collection.[4] The authors and senior members of the Associations provided cooperation, supervision and hospitality.

Opportunities to view the collections in person were provided by repeated attendance at the Gion Festival procession itself during the years 1993–2001. I also viewed multiple rotating exhibitions installed in the Kyoto Cultural Property Exhibition Room at Sakura Bank, then near the headquarters of the Associations in downtown Kyoto. I was also given opportunities to review retired textiles stored in Kyoto City's Research and Preservation Hall. In addition, helpful local private individuals provided access to collections that included comparable examples.

My textile interests up to this time had been wide ranging. In the 1970s and 1980s I had opportunities to study several collections of American and European textiles, travelling to Mexico, Western and Eastern Europe, collecting examples and attending classes and lectures. My husband's research on environmental health problems had enabled me repeatedly to visit countries in Eastern Europe. A conference in Poland startled me by revealing the amazing contemporary weavings produced in that land. Although Polish towns were still recuperating from World War II, our hosts showed me impressive family embroideries strung along the walls of their apartments, and superb kilims on their floors. In the rest of Europe pile carpets were de rigeur, and I had always been drawn to them. At a conference in Oaxaca, Mexico, I was introduced to the charm of the brocaded cotton garments called *huipiles*.

As I travelled and studied, attending multiple courses, textile conferences, and exhibitions in the United States, I found myself drawn repeatedly to Asian textile design. The need to understand Asian cultures led me to enroll in Japanese language and culture courses, and eventually I was impelled to return to UCLA to obtain my Master's degree. Throughout the 1980s and 1990s I travelled annually to Japan, conducting research and creating collections of Japanese textiles, which were acquired by American and European institutions (or gifted to them). In the early 1980s I began serving as museum curator at the Los Angeles Craft and Folk Art Museum, curating Asian textile exhibitions. In 1994 I produced the catalogue *Splendor of the Dragon: Costumes of the Ryukyuan Kingdom.* I returned again to UCLA as a Research Associate in the 1990s, and in 2002 I curated the exhibition and produced the catalogue *Matsuri! Japanese Festival Arts,* at the Fowler Museum at UCLA.

The 1994 Japan Foundation Grant led me to decades of investigation and documentation, both within Japan and also in China. At that time I became aware of two unidentified groups of wool textiles — ink-painted tapestries and knotted-pile carpets — stored in the Kyoto treasure houses. Dissatisfied with the 'Korean' labels assigned to them, I determined to spend a few months finding their true identity.

Convinced that the answers lay in China, I went north, travelling along the river roads, knowing that rivers served as the great freeways for China before the modern age. Since there was proof of ink-painted tapestries being used in northern Japan, I headed to art institutions and carpet-making workshops in China's northern provinces of Heilongjiang, Jilin and Liaoning. North Korea presented barriers to investigation that I did not feel I could surmount, despite the Kyotoites' devotion to the theory that the mystery textiles came from Korea.

When my investigations in the north proved fruitless, I wondered about China's south. Very occasionally antique dealers in Japan and in the United States, and also international auction houses, had offered examples of what appeared to be tapestries related to the Kyoto painted wool pieces.

These were thinner and newer than those stored in Japan and were reportedly produced from the seventeenth to twentieth centuries in towns along the Yangtse River (see chapter 11). They did not provide much insight into the provenance of the weavings stored in Japan.

Back home I again reviewed the colour transparencies of the Kyoto material and read extensively about Chinese minority costume. In addition to motifs that I had, through my research, come to think of as Manichaean, there were multiple motifs that were undoubtedly Tibetan Buddhist in origin. It then occurred to me that the river traffic that should have been investigated was that of the Yellow River, which rises in Tibet and flows through Qinghai and Gansu in northwest China, where it is the site of multiple Tibetan Buddhist communities.

Thus in 1997 I began what was to become more than a decade of exploring temples, towns and wool-weaving workshops in the Yellow River Valley, along a little-known northeastern branch of the Silk Road. It was here, for the first time in my travels, that motifs related to the textiles in Japan, and that I now thought of as Manichaean in origin, began to appear on buildings, and particularly on local costume.

Gloria Gonick, Los Angeles 2015

NOTES

1. F. Crawford Burkitt, *The Religion of the Manichees* (1925): 11–16. Jes Peter Asmussen, *Manichaean Literature: Representative Texts Chiefly from Middle Persian and Parthian Writings* (1975): 6.
2. For a description of the religion's history and proscriptions against it in China see: Lieu, Samuel N.C., *Manichaeism in the Later Roman Empire and Medieval China*, Tubingen, Germany, J.C. Mohr (Paul Siebeck) 2 edition, revised and expanded. (1992): 234–304.
3. Gonick, 'Foreign Textiles', 19–23; Gloria Granz Gonick, *Matsuri! Japanese Festival Arts* (2002).
4. Nobuko Kajitani and Kojiro Yoshida, *Gion Matsuri Yamaboko Kensohin Chosa Hokokusho: Torai Senshokuhin no Bu* [Catalogue of the Gion Festival float decorations: the imported hangings] (Kyoto: Gion Matsuri Yamaboko Rengokai, 1992, in Japanese).

1 'FOREIGN' TEXTILES IN KYOTO

Kyoto's big midsummer Gion Festival, a Shinto-Buddhist spectacle, began in the eighth century when the city was Japan's capital and continues to the present day. The festival (*matsuri*) honours the Japanese deities (*kami*) believed to have bestowed prosperity and fame on the city. Gion Temple, also known by its Shinto designation, Yasaka Shrine, is the host of the event. On the day of the festival bedecked festival wagons, accompanied by singers, musicians and dancers in bold summer kimono, are pulled through the streets of downtown Kyoto, which are crowded with spectators [1.2]. In the 1300s civil unrest caused temporary cancellation of the festival and fires destroyed many of the wagons and their decorations. After a lapse, several were rebuilt and, festooned with their surviving hangings, they reappeared around the year 1500 CE [1.4].[5]

In the decades preceding the wagons' reappearance, imported goods began to find their way into the coffers of Kyoto's merchant community. The imports entered Japan as a consequence of the newly established transoceanic trade. Although

1.1
Detail, Painted Tapestry No.79. Cooperating guardian dogs on Light and Dark ground. Courtesy Kanko Boko Association.

1.2

12

1.2
Screen painting. The festival carts, their sides draped with painted tapestries, are depicted in procession. Scenes in and around Kyoto, Edo Period (1603–1868 CE), Gion Matsuri Daiten (Gion Festival Exhibition), Courtesy Kyoto City Culture Museum, 1994.

the goods were originally bestowed on people in power (i.e. the samurai lords) to secure trading privileges, gifts selected by European adventurers often had minimal appeal to Japanese taste. Many luxury goods became donations to Buddhist temples, eventually to be turned over to neighbourhood festival organisations. It was illegal for the samurai to engage openly in commerce, but some objects were surreptitiously sold.

The artworks entered Japan through three ports of entry: in the South through Naha in the Ryukyu Islands (Okinawa); through Nagasaki, the centre of the lively European-Chinese-Japanese trade; and through a 'Northern Silk Route', which conveyed goods through the land and sea lanes of the Ainu tribes.[6] Kyoto curio dealers also travelled to port cities, acquiring goods in exchange for Japanese silk and silver.[7]

THE KYOTO COLLECTIONS

Many of the festival's foreign imports originated in China, but they also came from India, Central Asia and the Middle East, and as far away as Europe.[8] These were the treasures brought to Japan through

the ages to curry favour with the Japanese emperor, the samurai lords and wealthy merchants. Included among the gifts were bales of luxury fabrics, thick carpets and lavish costumes. When they arrived in Japan their appearance astonished the Japanese. The residents of the Japanese Archipelago had never encountered such vibrant shades of red, abundant gold embroidery or amazing images. Since the purpose of the festival procession was to honour and astonish the Japanese *kami*, perceived as otherworldly spirits, the Kyoto parade organisers were pleased with their newfound means of establishing what appeared to be a supernatural atmosphere.

The imported festival trappings, eventually numbering around 1,200 objects, would continue to arrive in Japan intermittently over the next five centuries. During that span the treasures have been stored and maintained by each of the thirty-two Gion Festival Associations participating in the festival. Trappings deemed suitable for display are retrieved from each Association headquarters a few days before the annual procession of floats on 17 July, and replaced at the end of that day.[9] The event is currently

1.3

viewed each year by tens of thousands of cheering spectators from all over Japan and also by international visitors.

In the early years of research in Kyoto, the Associations in the Sakura Bank Building maintained an exhibition gallery. In this gallery the space was rotated among the member Associations, each participating Association hanging or displaying its treasures in glass cases for around a month. These exhibitions, which I was able to visit on several occasions, provided yet another opportunity to study the material up close, and to view it in a stationary setting. In the gallery I was able to gather information from the labels, and discuss examples with the exhibition officials as well as with Japanese colleagues. Since textiles exhibitions are carefully scheduled to avoid undue exposure to light, the rotations in this gallery were strictly enforced, as were other regulations protective of humidity and temperature changes. With the exception of this gallery's examples and a few hangings displayed in members' meeting houses, the weavings have to be viewed in motion, albeit slow motion, as the draped festival floats are wheeled down the main streets of the city.

Below the ladders leading into the members' storerooms, the hot July streets are thickly packed with curious and enthusiastic onlookers. In orderly Japan, the disorderly but enthusiastic crowd strives to take in the view and be entertained in the spirit of what Yo-ichiro Hakomori describes as 'euphoric celebration'. Prof. Hakomori notes that some have described the mood, the excitement, the clamour and the crowds as comparable to New Orleans Mardi Gras (an event with entirely different origins).[10]

In Kyoto, groups of robed musicians stroll the streets and perch on the floats, practising for the next day's performance of traditional *matsuri* music, continuously sounding cymbals, drums, flutes and triangles. Festival songs are chorused over and over by the participants and many of the packed onlookers. The musicians and singers on the street and perched on the floats above wear *yukata*, lightweight cotton robes usually dyed or printed white and blue, sometimes accented with red or yellow. Many of the spectators also wear *yukata*, considered the most appropriate festival dress. The *yukata* are secured with bright red, gold or yellow *matsuri obi* wound around the waist. Onlookers include men, women, elders and children of all ages, who form a thick, moving procession snaking along Kyoto's downtown streets. The procession stops momentarily when one or more of the participants indicates his intention to pause – or sometimes to enter an accessible float. The Associations members continuously provide impressive and highly visible security.

Adding to the clamour, food purveyors continuously and loudly call out their offerings. The scents wafting up from barbecue stands and open sake jugs are near overwhelming as viewers, seemingly more eager to view the treasures than to replenish their bodies, push, shove and manoeuvre toward the floats. Everywhere it is extremely hot, humid, noisy and exciting.

In the cool, quiet streets of the city, away from the scene of the festival procession, can be found a sizable and secure research and preservation locker belonging to the City of Kyoto. The Kyoto Shi Rekishi Shiryokan holds retired trappings, hangings deemed unsuitable to be further exposed to the elements. In the weeks following the festival, I was privileged to gain entry to the large and sombre structure (under the close supervision of Association and City officials) and to spend hours viewing, inspecting and documenting the extremely old and rare examples of the weavers and dyers' accomplishments. Japanese society treasures fresh and pristine condition; it appeared that the distressed state of these textiles allowed their caretakers to feel somewhat relaxed about their being handled by an outsider (hands shielded continuously by fresh white cotton gloves).

1.3
A pile carpet from the 'mystery' group on the front of the Iwatori Association float during the annual Gion Festival.

1.4

1.4
Detail, The Gion Festival, painting on cedar door showing a cart draped with carpet hangings. Attributed to Sumiyoshi Gukai. 1600-1700 CE, Shoren-in, Kyoto.

For a researcher it was a heavenly opportunity. It is often in timeworn, malleable fragments that one can more easily examine the ground weave, the knotting, the ply of the yarns, and even the blurred outlines of abandoned motifs. Most of the textiles could clearly be related to specific regional traditions, including European tapestries, Persian and Turkish carpets, Indian printed cottons, and Chinese silk embroideries and brocades.

In addition to the objects themselves, written records beginning from the seventeenth century were extant for many items. Several Associations maintain handwritten record books of members' donations to acquire or repair the hangings. Commentary, paintings and sketches, and eyewitness accounts are also preserved. Numerous historians and artists, as well as dedicated members of the Associations, had studied the material over the centuries, many recording their thoughts. During the twentieth century several foreign scholars were invited to come to Kyoto to examine and document the carpets, bringing with them conventional western methods of describing carpet characteristics and proposing age and origins.

In the Associations' records the provider
of the artwork was never documented, as that
information might have been problematic.
During the Edo Period, trade between China
and Japan was regulated by both governments.
Many of the Gion artworks were collected
during years when importation of foreign
goods was strictly illegal in Japan. However,
Korea and the Ryukyu Islands (Okinawa)
had a quasi-tributary relationship with Japan,
so the restrictions were modified on their
imports. If artwork came from Korea or
the Ryukyus it would not automatically be
outright contraband.

Most of the 400 'foreign' textiles could
be identified following the investigation at
the Research and Preservation facility, the
inspection of the hangings in the members'
headquarters, the viewing during festival
preparation, and the festival itself. There
were, however, two groups that defied firm
classification by Japanese as well as foreign
scholars. These were a group of thirty-six
ink-painted wool tapestries [1.1] and a group
of twenty-one wool-pile carpets [1.3, 1.4].
The effort to uncover their provenance was
the impetus for this book.

NOTES

5. Kojiro Yoshida,
'The Gion Festival and
Imported Draperies',
*Bulletin of International
Research Center for Japanese
Studies* 9 (1993): 80.
6. Gloria Granz
Gonick, 'Foreign
Textiles at the Gion
Festival', *The Japan
Foundation Newsletter* 22,
No.4 (1995): 19–23.
7. Charles Ralph Boxer,
*Portuguese Merchants and
Missionaries in Feudal Japan,
1543–1640*, Collected
Studies Series CS 232
(London: Variorum
Reprints, 1986);
K. Ohtsuka, *Ainu Moshiri:
Minzoku Mon'you kara Mita
Ainu no Sekai* [The world of
the Ainu through their
design motifs] (1993):
60–61.
8. Gonick, 'Foreign
Textiles', (1995): 19–23.
9. At present the
Associations hold a
procession on two dates
in July, in accord with
early tradition.
10. Yo-ichiro
Hakomori, 'The Sacred
and the Profane in
Matsuri Structures', in
Matsuri! Japanese Festival Arts
(2002): 77.

2

HISTORICAL, RELIGIOUS AND CULTURAL CONTEXT

The Uyghurs left their original homeland in Mongolia in the eighth century and dispersed southward to sites east and west. The largest and most powerful colony was established in far western China, in and around Turfan, in the region known today as Xinjiang. This highly productive group of refugees, arriving in an area of rich resources, thrived, developed urban centres, and achieved notable literary and artistic accomplishments.

Beginning in the eighth century the Uyghurs practised the 'Religion of Light', or Manichaeanism, a belief system founded by the philosopher Mani. The designs on both the pile carpets and the ink-painted tapestry artefacts preserved in Japan in the Kyoto storerooms reflect the words of Mani. This is similar to the manner in which Christian ecclesiastical textiles celebrate the story of Christ. It also evokes the Buddhist practice of weaving emblems pertaining to the life of Buddha on to textiles. In addition to the Manichaean imagery on the ink-painted tapestries and pile carpets stored in Kyoto, there are also references to Tibetan Buddhism, and later to Taoism as well as

2.1
Detail, Pile Carpet No.44, Fig. 3.20. The Tree of Life shelters the White Tiger, whose eyes glare from deep-set sockets and heavily outlined lids. Courtesy Kanko Boko Preservation Association.

2.2

2.2

Landscape of the Yellow River territory.

Manichaeanism. However, on the ink-painted tapestries and the pile carpets, the oldest themes and most prevalent icons are Manichaean.

Pockets of Manichaean believers inhabited regions of Western China from the eighth century (762 CE) onward.[11] The Manichaean religion was the official state religion of the Uyghur peoples from the eighth century, purportedly dying out in China sometime between the fifteenth and seventeenth centuries. Manichaean relics uncovered in the Turfan region dating from the eighth to the eleventh centuries are widely known and preserved in several institutions. They were described in the twentieth century by Grünwedel (1912), Le Coq (1928), Stein (1933), Klimkeit (1977, 1982), Lieu (1977, 1985) and Moriyasu (1991). Further documentation in the twenty-first century has been provided by Moriyasu (2001), Russell-Smith (2005), Gulácsi (2001, 2005) and Bhattacharya-Haesner (2005). However, the Manichaean relics produced in Gansu and Qinghai provinces,[12] to the east of the Turfan discoveries, have been largely ignored. This volume will attempt to describe some of those relics.

MANICHAEAN ARTEFACTS

Manichaean artefacts are most often associated with the late nineteenth- and early twentieth-century finds in and around Turfan and Beshbalik in far western China. The dry desert climate of those locales meant that murals, textiles and illustrated books survived for centuries. Elsewhere in China such objects were often demolished or destroyed, victims of climatic extremes or extremist human trespassers. In the dark caves where recognisable relics have been uncovered, they have been protected from light as well as moisture, thanks to the efforts of the pious and dedicated monks who entombed them. The monks' devotion prevented marauders or zealots of competing faiths from imposing total destruction.

The surviving artefacts were eventually uncovered by a number of energetic, mostly European explorers, beginning around 1890. Their investigations continued until the advent of World War II in the late 1930s, which brought their probing to a halt for several decades.[13] These explorers, scholars and adventurers of international origins include Sir Marc Aurel Stein of England, Sven Hedin of Sweden, Nikolai Przhevalsky and Sergei Oldenburg of Russia, Otani Kozui of Japan, Paul Pelliot of France, Albert von Le Coq and Albert Grünwedel of Germany. Each possessed a distinct set of motives, which included adventure, archaeology, treasure hunting and fame.[14] The publicity accompanying the news of their discoveries excited art historians as well as artists worldwide.

Since World War II scholars have had to focus their attention on the surviving relics from these finds bestowed by Aurel Stein on the British Museum and the National Museum, New Delhi. Many objects are also preserved at the Asian Art Museum, Berlin. Scholarly reports on Manichaean relics and documents, publications that picture and describe Uyghur textiles and costumes, as well as illustrated manuscripts, have been published by, among others, Hans-Joachim Klimkeit, Annemarie von Gabain, Takao Moriyasu and Zsuzsanna Gulácsi. Chhaya Bhattacharya-Haesner has catalogued the painted banners from Turfan. Lilla Russell-Smith has described Uyghur Manichaean paintings and drawings of the ninth to eleventh centuries found in Dunhuang, and has analysed their styles and influences.

THE YELLOW RIVER REGION

Despite this worthy bibliography, the intense focus on the Turfan and Dunhuang sites and their resulting elevated status in academia has seemingly prevented scholars from looking at other regions of China that hosted Uyghur Manichaean communities. This book seeks to remedy the omission and remove the barriers to investigating the other fertile sites. Scholars will need to abandon the idea that only written documents and paintings provide information; in China's Gansu and Qinghai provinces they need to reap the riches bestowed by cultural artefacts.

Far east of Turfan, beginning in the ninth century, the Uyghur Manichaeans established communities all along the Yellow River and its tributaries in what are now Gansu and Qinghai provinces. These Uyghurs, still practising their religion, undoubtedly mixed with remnants of the ancient Xianbei population that had inhabited the sparsely populated region. The Uyghurs pledged allegiance to the conquering Mongols in 1209. Gradually, the mixed Uyghur population would mate with the Mongol soldiers led by General Subutai, a favourite commander of Genghis Khan. The descendants of these unions became known as Monguors.[15] The temples, textiles, and the paintings and sculpture they bequeathed to the area reveal today their Uyghur Manichaean inheritance, and provide a unique, mostly unexplored body of art.

2.3

2.3
Landscape of the Yellow River territory.

2.4
Map of the Yellow River region showing, in red, the northeastern branch of the Silk Road. See also fig.4.13

Unfortunately, in addition to the real Great Wall running horizontally across northern China, there seems to be an imaginary wall perpendicular to the actual one. It swoops down and cuts the Yellow River region off from the well-publicised sites in Turfan, Bezeklik and Dunhuang.

Archaeological exploration of the Yellow River territory appears almost non-existent, even though today it takes no more than hours to go beyond the many well-travelled and documented sites. Political, climatic or geographic barriers should no longer be a reason to ignore this important repository of material culture.

There is also human resistance to exploration of the region. When it was announced in 1998 that a research trip would be undertaken to northwest China to try to find the production sites of the material preserved in Japan, both Chinese and foreigners reacted negatively. They expressed extreme scepticism and advised abundant caution. There were warnings of a wild environment, one that included bandits and tigers. It was implied that a naive foreign scholar would probably encounter an uncooperative and somewhat rude,

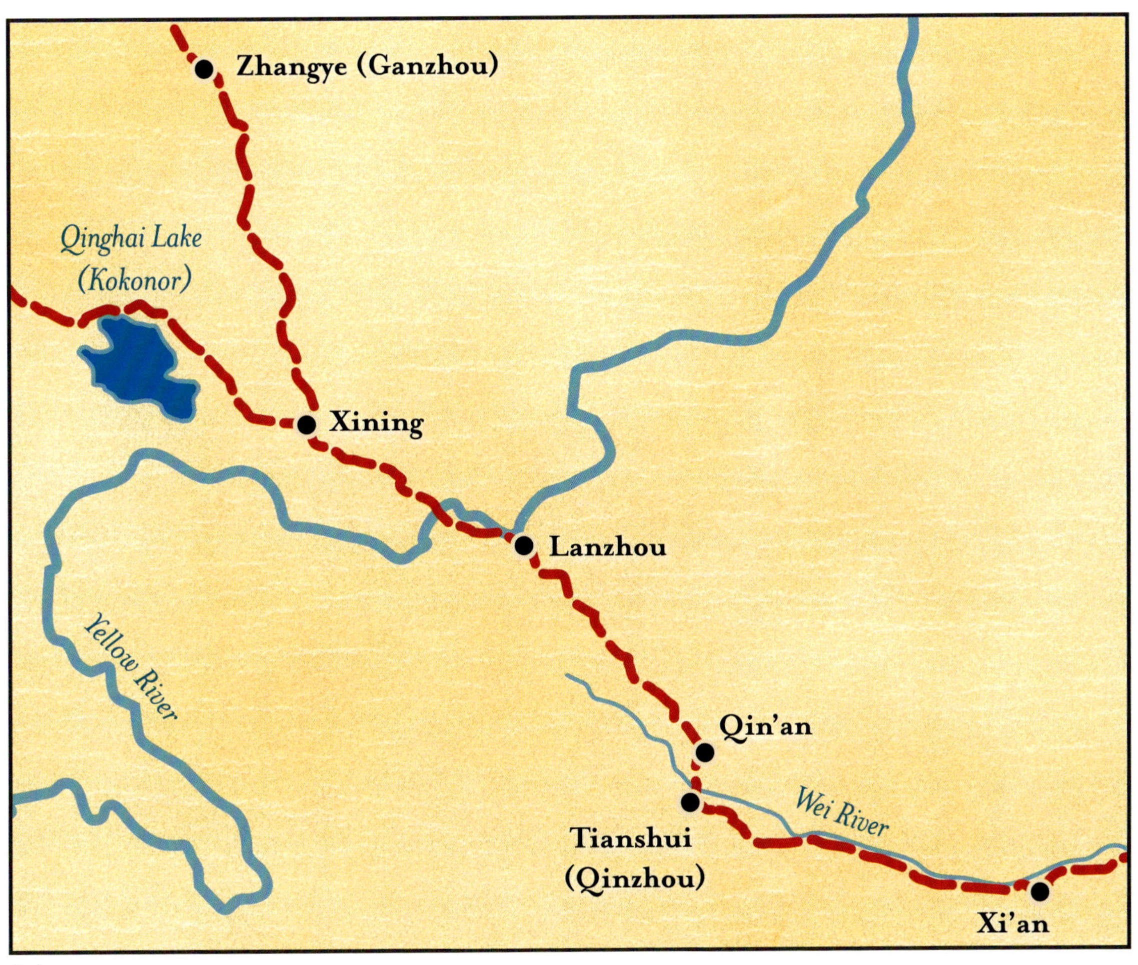

2.4

uncivilised population that might actually lead a visitor to harm. Much propaganda was put out implying that the area was devoid of interest. The Chinese government does not welcome visitors to an area that it believes harbours the descendants of Uyghurs, perceived in China as a continuously troublesome component of the Chinese population.

I hope that the friendship, help and guidance I received, as shown in this volume, will indicate the true civility and pride of the resident populations of Gansu and Qinghai.

NOTES

11. Luciano Petech, in Rossabi, *China among Equals*, 1983: 100, 173–77, 254–57; Johann Elverskog, *Uyghur Buddhist literature* (1997): 6–7; Michael R. Drompp, *Tang China and the Collapse of the Uighur Empire: A Documentary History* (2005).

12. Gansu and Qinghai were one province called Gansu until 1928.

13. Peter Hopkirk, *Foreign Devils on the Silk Road: The Search for the Lost Cities and Treasures of Chinese Central Asia* (1980): 210

14. Irene M. Franck and David M. Brownstone, *The Silk Road: A History* (1986): 270–75.

15. Henry G. Schwarz, *The Minorities of Northern China: A Survey* (1984): 107–109. See Schram, Louis M. J., *The Monguors of the Kansu–Tibetan Frontier*, Transactions of the American Philosophical Society 51 (Philadelphia: American Philosophical Society, 1957):

3 The Mystery Collections

There are fifty-seven textiles in the Gion Festival Associations' collection that have until now been of uncertain provenance: thirty-six ink-painted wool tapestries and twenty-one wool-pile carpets. The Associations' catalogue divides the two mystery groups. It declares the ink-painted tapestries to have originated in Korea, calling them 'Chosen ke tsutsure', or Korean wool tapestries. Seoul, Korea lies over 2,000 kilometres east of China. The pile carpets are designated 'Chinese Regional', referring to a nebulous site over 3,000 kilometres in the opposite direction, somewhere along the western border of China.[16]

However, the evidence indicates that both groups of textiles, although serving two distinct functions, were produced by the same people or by people living in neighbouring communities. According to the records, examples of both types entered the Associations around the same time and were acquired by the same member Associations. A similar wool fibre was used in both groups, although the carpet fibre is hairier than that used in the ink-painted tapestries and some carpets are significantly more coarsely woven. Many of the

3.1
Paired peacocks. Detail of Fig.3.12, Ink-Painted Tapestry No.60. Courtesy Niwatori Boko Preservation Association.

juǎn cǎo wén

3.2

3.3

3.4

3.5

26

3.2
*Chinese characters for the
Curly Grass motif.*

3.3
*The Curly Grass motif.
This distinctive curvilinear
motif, known in China as the
'Curly Grass' motif appears on
the surface of the ink-painted
tapestries and also on the pile
carpets.*

motifs that appear on the ink-painted tapestries
may also be seen on the pile carpets.

Clues leading to an understanding of
the provenance of textile or carpet artworks
include: identifying the main fibre or fibres
used to create the object; determining the
technique or techniques employed to create the
wool yarn itself; and discovering the method of
combining the warp and weft to produce the
fabric. In addition, an investigator notes any
common colour palette selected, determines the
dyes employed, the typical manner of finishing
any borders or hems, and notes any consistent
painting or surface designs, if they exist.

THE INK-PAINTED TAPESTRIES

The more mystifying of the two puzzling
collections in Kyoto is the group of
thirty-six ink-painted tapestries. Seeing
an example for the first time, one might
imagine one is looking at a twentieth-
century painting, perhaps a Jean Miró or
an unfamiliar Picasso work. Yet the works
are documented to have been in storage in
Kyoto for nearly 500 years. Any attempt to
discern the artist's intention, or to associate
the design with something one has seen
before, is to no avail. Beyond the painting
the intended function of the textile is also a

3.7

3.6

3.4

Detail, Ink-Painted Tapestry No.74. The outlined square contains Curly Grass motifs. These also surround the peacock and other auspicious birds, outlined in black ink. Birds, a favourite Uyghur motif, often appear on the ink-painted tapestries. In addition to the peacock in a variety of poses and images, multiple cranes and magpies are seen on this example amid broad-leaved foliage. They appear on a background design of vertical segments of light and dark hues. Courtesy Houka Boko Preservation Association.

3.5

Annemarie von Gabain documented spiral designs in her book on early Uyghur art. She terms this image 'Spiral scroll motif'. Gabain, 1973, Das Lebe, 235, fig. 83.

3.6

Detail, spiral motif on dark background segment, Ink-Painted Tapestry No.73. Along with The Curly Grass motifs ink-painted in numerous formations, spiral motifs also appear frequently on the ink-painted tapestries. The spiral motif on No.73 is ink-drawn on a 'Dark' vertical segment. Courtesy Houka Boko Association.

3.7

Detail, Ink-Painted Tapestry No.70. The White Tiger's face, body, limbs and tail are composed of Curly Grass motifs and other curvilinear forms. In Uyghur drawing and painting, there appears to be an abhorence of straight lines. Courtesy Kanko Boko Preservation Association.

3.8

mystery; the weavings do not seem to serve as an obvious cover, curtain, or a costume element. The dimensions and design layout do not seem to suggest a specific use.

Materials and Technique

The fibre employed almost universally in the creation of the materials in the ink-painted tapestries is sheep's wool. The tapestries and the pile carpets preserved in Kyoto are woven of a superior quality wool, possibly the fluffy white long-fibre variety described and illustrated by Rostov and Jia, who note that superior wool is produced by the Tanyang or Tibetan sheep traditionally herded in China's Gansu and Qinghai provinces. It is considered ideal for making carpets and garments.[17] The strong wool used is sheared from sheep living only in the very cold Qinghai-Tibet Plateau, 3,000 metres above sea level. The wool is long-fibre, of strong tension, bright lustre and excellent resilience. A few of the pile carpets also include cotton, hair and even rag in their construction.

The ink-painted tapestries were made by a method known to weavers simply as 'tapestry'. Although the Sogdian people

3.9

3.10

3.11

3.8
Ink–Painted Tapestry No.77. Vertical segments of Light and Dark (safflower red, brown, and gold) provide a background for curvilinear forms of deep indigo–accented peacocks, peonies, cranes and bold curving leaves. This tapestry is woven of dyed wool yarns with outlining and detailing in black ink. Warp: 9 warps per 2.5 cm. Weft: 32 wefts per 2.5 cm. 158 x 85 cm. Courtesy Houka Boko Preservation Association.

3.9
Detail, Ink–Painted Tapestry No.76. Apricot blossoms appear to float on the surface and surround the protective white tiger. Curly Grass and floral motifs appear between the Light and Dark stripes. Courtesy Tsuki Boko Preservation Association.

3.10
Ink–Painted Tapestry No.58. Considered the oldest by the Associations, this tapestry depicts a blossoming Tree of Life on a ground of Light and Dark segments. In this example the safflower red has oxidized to a shade of gold. Warp: 10 warps per 2.5 cm. Weft: 44 wefts per 2.5 cm. 170 x 104 cm. Courtesy Naginata Boko Preservation Association.

3.11
Detail, Ink–Painted Tapestry No.59. Courtesy Kanko Boko Preservation Association.

30 3.12
Ink–Painted Tapestry No.60. Paired peacocks and peonies surround the sun, considered a Manichaean deity.[25] *The clouds encircling the sun are clusters of delicate Curly Grass motifs. Above the paired peacocks a blossoming branch of the 'Tree of Life' is seen. Warp: 13 warps per 2.5 cm. Weft: 28 wefts per 2.5 cm. 175 x 124 cm. Courtesy Niwatori Boko Preservation Association.*

3.12

3.13

are generally credited with having invented tapestry technique, the Uyghurs are thought to have conveyed the skill to China. In the ink-painted tapestries the coloured pictorial elements in the basic ground weave were laid out first, then woven together and connected to the background according to the carefully predetermined plan of their master designers. The elements were attached to adjacent foundation elements with connective weaving techniques, sometimes augmented by means of painting techniques. In Uyghur tapestry weaving the pictorial components are usually outlined and elaborated in dark black ink. This black outlining feature appears on the ink-painted tapestries preserved in Kyoto.

Since very similar images appear on several of these tapestries it is thought that cartoons might have been employed for some examples. The tapestry technique used to create the ink-painted tapestries indicates that the entire design and colour blocks were planned and the batch of selected yarns laid out on a flat surface in accord with the plan of the designer. The yarns were then tapestry woven on a simple handloom. After the major colour areas were woven in, another or

3.13

Detail of Ink-Painted Tapestry No. 75. Cranes, magpies, the peacock and the peony connote auspicious tidings. Courtesy Iwato Yama Preservation Association.

31

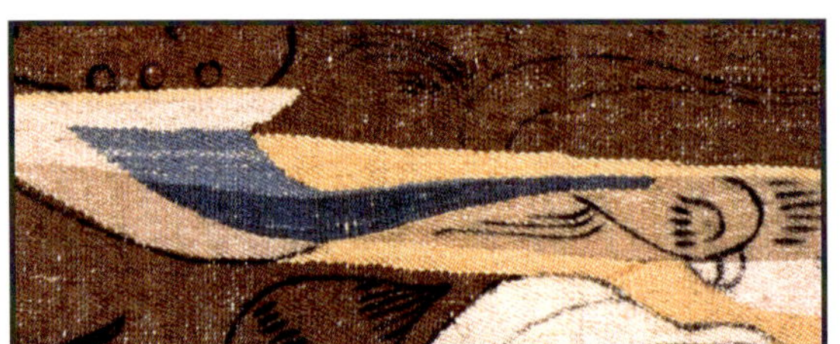

3.14b Peacock

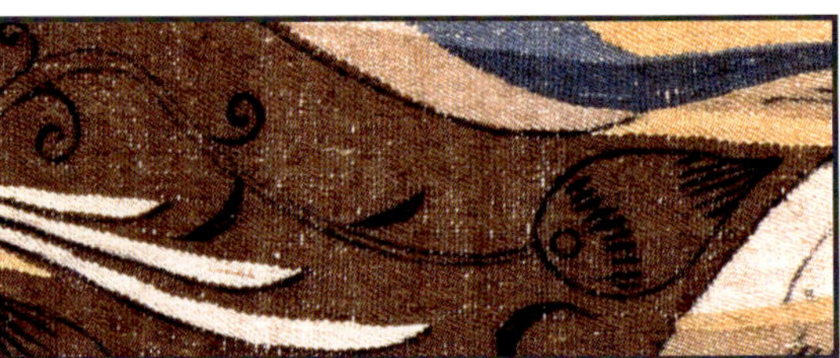

3.14e Lotus Bud

3.14c Forked Branch

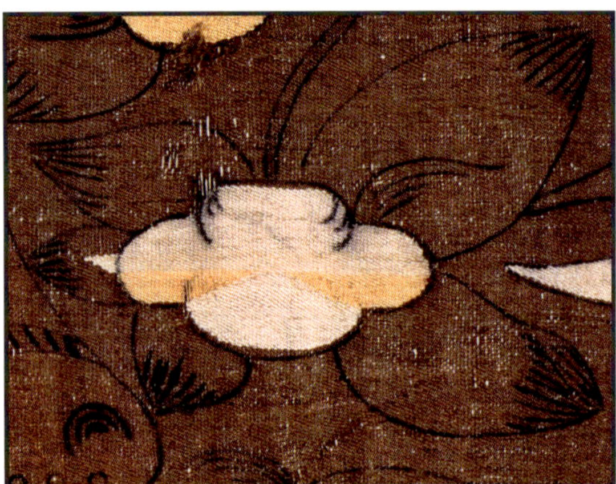

3.14d Peony

3.14f Jellyfish

32

possibly the same artisan skilfully enhanced the images, judiciously drawing in outlines and accents with pen and black ink directly on the multicoloured wool surface.

It is known that Uyghur tapestry painters and weavers preferred the pen to the brush.[18] On many of the tapestries the details are created and defined by a series of very thin parallel black lines, in keeping with Uyghur painting traditions. In addition to the main and auxiliary near-recognisable forms, a variety of isolated and joined curvilinear shapes — including 'curly grass' motifs, spirals and curlicues — may be seen in the interstices of broad stripes.

Design and Motifs

A particularly distinctive curvilinear motif, identified in China as the 'curly grass' motif [3.2, 3.3] appears repeatedly on the surface designs of the ink-painted tapestries and also appears on the pile carpets. This mysterious motif shows prominently on twenty-three out of the thirty-six ink-painted tapestry examples, suggesting that the makers regarded its inclusion as quite important. The motif is said to have originated in Central Asia, and is discussed further in Chapter 7.

Another clue indicative of Uyghur participation in the creation of these

3.15

3.16

3.17

3.14a–f *(and detail overleaf) Ink–Painted Tapestry No.68. Transcendence was of great interest to Manichaeans and butterflies and tadpoles are tapped for images. A translucent jellyfish appears on this ink–painted tapestry. Courtesy Tsuki Boko Preservation Association.*

3.15 *Detail, Ink–Painted Tapestry No.74. In this late ink–painted tapestry, created after Taoist images became more prevalent, an image of Mt. Horai, a site sacred to Taoists, is seemingly fused to a bird portrait. There are multiple Buddhist and Taoist influences in the Gion Festival itself and these are reflected in the hangings selected to adorn the festival. Courtesy Houka Boko Preservation Association.*

3.16 *Ink–Painted Tapestry No.70. The White Tiger is a talismanic creature in northwest China, thought to protect the inhabitants and their crops from hail and other dangers.*[26] *This White Tiger is surrounded by Curly Grass motifs and auspicious birds. Courtesy Tsuki Boko Preservation Association.*

3.17 *Detail and join, Ink–Painted Tapestries Nos. 70, 92. In order to drape the entire side of a Kyoto festival wagon, two or more ink–painted tapestries or carpets might be joined, frequently utilising a fragment from a 'retired' tapestry, or from a 'retired' carpet, as here. There are no complete surviving pile carpets with this archaic geometric design in the collections, but the now–vanished carpets can be imagined from this preserved segment used as a join.*

33

3.18

36

weavings is the overwhelming profusion of bird motifs, historically of great spiritual significance to the Uyghur people.[19] Multiple peacocks, cranes, doves, magpies and ducks are tapestry-woven and ink-drawn on the surface of most of the tapestries. The frequency with which birds are depicted dwindles, then disappears, in later examples.

'Curly grass' motifs, as well as flora and fauna, show against consistent background designs of alternating segments of light and dark hues. These broad vertical segments or alternating vertical stripes are somewhat difficult to discern today, but they become

visible through modern computer imagery techniques, as well as magnification. This light and dark background design persists on many examples produced over hundreds of years, suggesting that the theme of duality may have been important to the makers. The 'dark' segments are created with red/ orange safflower dye, now often oxidised to a shade of brown. It seems that, after some mishaps, the dyers chose not to use black to create the 'dark'; perhaps they observed on the earliest examples that black dye in time destroys its wool host. Some loss of the design due to this phenomenon may be observed

3.19

3.18
Pile Carpet No.56. The outer border of Turkic guls encloses a lattice inner border of Tibetan design origin.
Warp: 8 warps per 2.5 cm.
Weft: 4 wefts per 2.5 cm. 199 x 129 cm. Courtesy Niwatori Boko Preservation Association.

3.19
Pile Carpet No.51. Two cooperating guardian dogs, of dark hues, run on a light gold ground, rotating a prayer cylinder. The dogs' manes are of Curly Grass motifs. Repeated thin black lines indicate bushy tails. Successive thin black lines are a commonly used Uyghur painting technique. Turkic guls fill the border of the carpet.
Warp: 9 warps per 2.5 cm.
Weft: 5 wefts per 2.5 cm. 172 x 108 cm. Courtesy Iwatori Yama Preservation Association.

on Ink-Painted Tapestry No.58 [3.10], said to be the earliest of the extant weavings. The pronounced reiteration of the dark (red/orange) and the light (off-white) bands of colour on all of the tapestries' backgrounds alerted me to a possible connection to a dualistic faith, such as Manichaeanism.

Scattered throughout the textiles' numerous curvy forms, whimsical images seem to appear. Some line drawings resemble plants or sea creatures; others call to mind the Disney characters Donald Duck or Mickey Mouse [3.11]! [20] Sometimes the lines of black ink unscroll, spiral down, or unwind over the background of rectangular broad segments, whose colours alternate between light and dark in what often appears an animated composition. Light segments are juxtaposed with dark. The lighter segments appear originally to have been off-white, the natural colour of the sheep's wool. The darker segments, now often brown to dark brown, dive in and out of the light background. These dark segments were once an attractive shade of bright red-orange attributed to the prized dye from the safflower plant, long cultivated in northern Gansu Province. This dye has been treasured in East Asia. Its soft red-orange hues are appealing to the eye and are deemed to flatter various shades of human skin especially well. In Japan as well as in China, safflower has been historically sought for dyeing costly silk garments. In Japan it is particularly valued for lining women's luxury under-kimono.

The earliest ink-painted tapestries are also distinguished by a consistent draping quality. When viewing early examples in the glass cases of the Kyoto Cultural Property Exhibition Room at Sakura Bank in 1994, I was surprised to find that some tapestries seemed malleable. In order to show the rectangular textile flat in its large glass case it was necessarily gathered up in places, showing this draping characteristic, suggestive of textiles woven for clothing. It is less apparent in later ink-painted tapestries, which have a heavier, blanket-like hand.

THE PILE CARPETS

The 'Chinese Regional' carpets preserved in the Gion Festival Associations Collections consist of twenty-one knotted wool pile carpets decorated with bird, animal and plant designs on backgrounds of yellow-gold. Many of the carpets illustrate a prayer cylinder or a section of a prayer cylinder.

Materials and Technique

The Kyoto carpets are predominantly wool of a hairy type typical of sheep raised in the Chinese provinces of Gansu and Qinghai. [21] Wool was considered heavy, scratchy and animal-like in Japan. Apart from the examples in the Gion Festival Collections, woollen fabric became familiar in the Japanese Archipelago only after the arrival of Europeans during the Edo Period (1600–1858 CE). Wool fibre and its accompanying odour in the apparel of the European merchant mariners did not endear the fabric to the Japanese. Not until the nineteenth century did the wearing of wool garments become established in Japan, and with it the occupation of shepherding.

Nevertheless, several older examples of the Kyoto-stored wool-pile carpets have both wool warps and wool wefts. Permission was given to remove fibres from four examples, [22] and radiocarbon dating of three of the carpets took place in 1994, producing dates consistent with historic events. Threads from one pile carpet yielded creation dates of 1293–1437 CE with 95% probability. Another pile carpet was dated 1293–1447 CE with 95% probability. The third pile carpet was dated 1387–1511 CE with 95% probability. [23] These were decades in which 'Living Buddhas' were being recognised and installed in Tibet and northwest China.

The carpets are woven using asymmetrical knots, open to the left. There are about ten warps every 2.5 cm. The cotton warps are Z-spun with a few S-spun, twisted Z-ply. (Two Z-spun cotton threads are twisted

3.20 **39**

Pile Carpet No. 44. The Tree of Life shelters the White Tiger, whose eyes glare from deep-set sockets and heavily outlined lids. The many-branched tree also appears in a delicate version painted on the wool surface of four of the Ink-Painted Tapestries. Warp: 7 warps per 2.5 cm. Weft: 3 wefts per 2.5 cm. 167 x 105 cm. Courtesy Kanko Boko Preservation Association.

3.21a Runic Letters

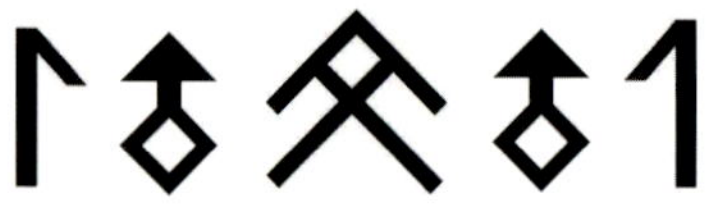

3.21b Runic Letters

3.21c Border Design

3.22

40

3.21a-c
Old Turkic runiform letters inspire the border design on four of the pile carpets.

S-ply). Several of the carpets are extremely coarse in weave, with as few as 78 knots per square decimetre. Some also seem to have been hastily assembled and possibly were woven by inexperienced rug makers. In later pieces, cotton was used as well as wool for the warps and the wefts. Occasionally other fibres, such as hair or hemp, were inserted in place of the wool or cotton yarns. In one case twisted cotton rags were used as wefts.

A limited palette was tapped. The colours usually include white, blue, yellow, brown and a shade of olive green.

Imagery and Function

Imagery on the carpets as well as on the tapestries was inspired by Manichaean, Buddhist, tribal and Taoist spiritual traditions. In East Asia, religion and religious artefacts are often syncretic. Multiple cultural ideas, time-honoured Turkic (Uyghur), Mongol and Tibetan Buddhist icons, all served the designers of the carpets. All the motifs are considered powerful, capable of affecting the well-being of the user as well as the viewer.

When elderly members of Monguor communities in Gansu were interviewed

3.23

3.24

3.22 (and detail overleaf)
Pile Carpet No. 47. 13th century.
Guardian dogs clutch ribbons
while rotating a prayer cylinder.
The geometric inner border
design appears on the dress of
the Monguor descendants of
Uyghur settlers and their Mongol
conquerors. The dark outer border
elements are runiform letters of the
Old Turkic alphabet, used by the
Uyghurs on religious objects after it
had been given up for vernacular
use.[27] Warp: 12 warps per 2.5 cm.
Weft: 6 wefts per 2.5 cm.
169 x 99 cm. Courtesy Naginata
Boko Preservation Association.

3.23
Prayer cylinders are a common
sight in the Monguor territories.
They are placed before temples
and monasteries, and also stand
alone. The cylinders are installed
on land and above rushing
streams, at times protected by a
roofed structure. In this example
rapid flowing waters rotate the
cylinder. The ability to disperse
the beneficence inscribed on their
prayers, had great importance
for the Uyghur Manichaeans.
After T. M. Ainscough, Notes
From A Frontier, Taipei:
1971, 65.

3.24
Chandling si (Ch), Chone
Monastery (Tb), Gansu
Province, China. Prayer
cylinders may be seen today
throughout regions populated by
Monguors and the surrounding
Tibetans in Northwest China.
There are several variations
in their design. The carpets
preserved in Kyoto portray a
top view of a prayer cylinder in
rotation. The top of the cylinder
pictured on these carpets
replaces the gem or the pearl
that appears on other Chinese
artworks.

3.25
Diagram of a prayer cylinder.
Images of prayer cylinders
appear on twelve of the twenty-
one pile carpets, depicted from
their top view. The cylinders
are intended to be perceived
as rotating, while being pulled
by cooperating guardian
dogs. Prayer cylinders appear
everywhere in northwest China
in a variety of forms.

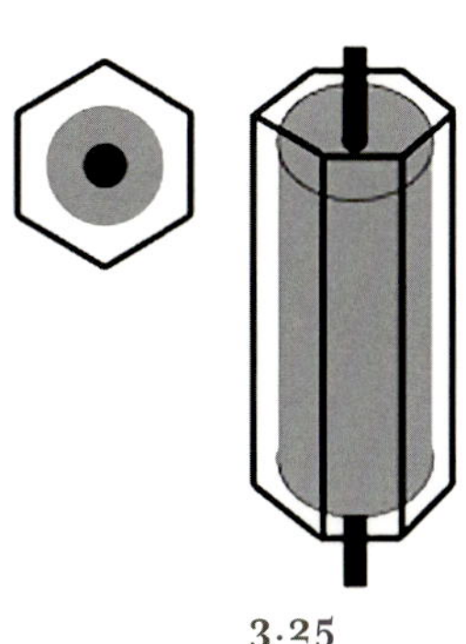

3.25

44

3.26
Pile Carpet No.40. Turkic guls (tribal insignia) alternate with swastikas and a running fret. This pattern alternates with a geometric design seen on the costumes of the Monguors, a Chinese minority. Old Turkic runiform letters inspire the outer border motif.
Warp: 14 warps per 2.5 cm.
Weft: 7 wefts per 2.5 cm.
177 x 99 cm. Courtesy Naginata Boko Preservation Association.

3.27

in 1998, they consistently identified the carpets as 'audience carpets' restricted to the use of Living Buddhas (*Hutukhtu*). A Living Buddha is a high lama who is believed to be the reincarnation of a bodhisattva who has achieved enlightenment but elects to live in the society of men to teach and serve them. The carpets provide a 'Seat of Authority' for a Living Buddha holding audience. Their consistent yellow ground colour reflects the ascendance of 'Yellow Hat' Buddhism at the time of the carpets' production in the fifteenth to sixteenth centuries.

The Mongols had converted from Shamanism to the Yellow Hat sect of Tibetan Buddhism. They offered their support to its leader, Lama Tsongkhapa (1357–1419 CE), who was born and raised in Gansu-Qinghai province. The Mongols found it useful to support the concept of the Living Buddha as they were attempting to consolidate their military gains in this region, with its significant Tibetan population.[24] One can speculate that the Mongols' decision to support the Yellow Sect and its Living Buddha institution might have occasioned a need for new and additional ceremonial trappings.

3.27

Pile Carpet No. 53. Guardian dogs pull a light and dark ribbon held between their teeth, turning a prayer cylinder as they run. Their manes are clusters of Curly Grass motifs. The inner border is based on Turkic gul (tribal insignia) designs and the outer border is a running fret motif. The slotted hexagon in the centre indicates the prayer cylinder. Warp: 7 warps per 2.5 cm. Weft: 5 wefts per 2.5 cm. 145 x 92 cm. Courtesy Tsuki Boko Preservation Association.

3.28

3.29

46

3.28

A Living Buddha holds audience in the early 20th century. He is installed and flanked by wool pile carpets with powerful protective motifs. Photo by Folke Bergman, in Henning Haslund, trans. Elizabeth Sprigge and Claude Napier, Men and Gods in Mongolia, *1935; reprint, Stelle, IL: Adventures Unlimited Press, 1992, 192.*

The carpets retain herdsmen's imagery, particularly the impressive rams' horns, thought to beget increasing herds, which do not appear on the ink-painted tapestries. The horns of Mongol sheep are particularly large and prominent.

Another motif, the three-trunked tree, each trunk forking once more, is sometimes called the Tree of Life. The apricot's three slender trunks have evolved in the Kyoto carpets into a tree with an abnormally thick curving trunk with a curiously squared-off base, above which three blossoming branches extend parallel to the dramatically curved trunk. On pile carpet No.42 [3.29] red-orange apricot fruits are portrayed on a curving branch.

It is likely that both the red-orange colour of the fruit and the curvilinear form of its branches made the apricot tree a particularly appealing image. The Uyghur and their descendants, the Monguor, particularly favoured red-orange hues.

3.29
Pile Carpet No.42. An apricot tree is depicted with a curving trunk, bending branches paralleling the trunk, and a surprisingly squared off base.[28 29 30] Warp: 12 warps per 2.5 cm. Weft: 6 wefts per 2.5 cm. 175 x 105 cm. Courtesy Naginata Boko Preservation Association.

NOTES

16. Nobuko Kajitani and Kojiro Yoshida, *Gion Matsuri,* (1992): 72–74, 84–85.

17. Charles I. Rostov and Jia Guanyan, *Chinese Carpets* (New York: Harry N. Abrams, 1983), 172, 175, 177, pl 109, 110.

18. Lilla Russell-Smith, *Uygur Patronage in Dunhuang: Regional Art Centres on the Northern Silk Road in the Tenth and Eleventh Centuries,* (2005): 114.

19. Usmanovna Risalat Karimova, 'Uighur Rugs: The Tradition of Figural Designs' in *Ghereh: International Carpet & Textile Review* 10, No.31 (2002): 12.

20. Gulácsi (2005) refers to this image as a tear-drop shape. Figure 4/1MIK 6265 NS MIK 4979 recto.

21. Charles I. Rostov and Jia Guanyan, *Chinese Carpets* (New York, Harry N. Abrams, 1983): 109, 110.

22. In collaboration with colleagues Alan Marcuson and Nicholas Purdon, then of HALI: *The International Magazine of Antique Carpet and Textile Art.*

23. University of Oxford Research Laboratory for Archaeology and the History of Art, Unpublished Report, 'Report on Radiocarbon Dating by Accelerator Mass Spectrometry,' May 5, 1995.

24. Schram, Louis M. J., *The Monguors of the Kansu–Tibetan Frontier,* vol. 2, *Their Religious Life,* Transactions of the American Philosophical Society 51 (Philadelphia: American Philosophical Society, 1957): 13.

25. Hans-Joachim Klimkeit, *Gnosis on the Silk Road: Gnostic Parables, Hymns & Prayers from Central Asia* (New York: HarperCollins, 1993), 227–52.

26. Usmanovna Risalat Karimova, 'Uighur Rugs: The Tradition of Figural Designs' in *Ghereh: International Carpet & Textile Review* 10, No.31 (2002): 12.

27. Schram, vol. 2: 97–99.

28. This carpet has been classified as Mongolian in a recent catalogue. The weavers of these carpets are not Mongols but the descendants of Uyghurs who mated with their Mongol conquerors in the twelfth century, giving rise to the Monguor people. Uyghur crafts include carpet weaving; Mongols are not themselves weavers, but acquire carpets from other peoples.

29. Igor de Rachewiltz and Volker Rybatzki with collaboration of Hung Chin-fu, *Introduction to Altaic Philology: Turkic, Mongolian, Manchu,* Handbook of Oriental Studies, Section Eight, Central Asia, Vol 20 (Brill. Leiden, The Netherlands 2010), 45-46, Figures 2, 3.

30. Talât Tekin, *A Grammar of Orkhon Turkic,* Uralic and Altaic Series 69. (Bloomington, IN: Indiana University Publications, 1968), 23–24.

4

THE SEARCH FOR PROVENANCE

A number of different provenances have been suggested for the ink-painted wool tapestries and wool-pile carpets in the Gion Festival Associations' collection, which have until now defied firm classification by Japanese as well as foreign scholars.

KOREA

The Japanese owners of the artworks have long considered Korea to be the source of the painted tapestries. They are convinced that the textiles entered Japan via the island of Tsushima, which lies between China and Japan and is primarily known in Japan as a port forwarding goods from Korea. A tag found on one of the tapestries read as 'to Tsushima'. However, in my estimation the artworks might have been forwarded via Korea and the port of Tsushima to Kyoto, but it is unlikely that they originated in Korea.

Koreans have traditionally not been interested in working with wool, utilising instead silk, grass (linen or ramie), or cotton fibres. A few examples of wool textiles came into Korea with Uyghur deputies accompanying the Mongol

Detail, Fig 4.4. The Teaching of Manichaeism and Other Narratives, late fourteenth century. In this painting, preserved in the Yamato Bunkakan, the white robed Manichaean priests wear a mantle or an overgarment. The Curly Grass motifs appear carved on the roof overhang.

4.2

4.2

Map: 'Early Carpets and Ink-Painted Tapestries: The Production Sites in China and The Routes of Importation to Japan.' By the tenth century, Uyghur refugees had settled in Xining and other communities along the Yellow River in Gansu Province.[59] *Courtesy Fowler Museum at UCLA; designed by the DLF Group.*

invaders in the thirteenth century. Since the Uyghurs were literate, the Mongols came to depend on them for accounting and administrative tasks.

Wool fabric did not become of interest to the Korean general public until the late nineteenth to early twentieth centuries.[31] The thirty-six woollen tapestries under discussion, preserved in Japan, arrived there intermittently over a more-than 350-year span, from approximately 1500 CE to around 1850 CE, suggesting they were made in a place where wool fabric production was continuous for a long time.

THE TIBETAN BUDDHIST REGIONS

A number of the images on the carpets and tapestries appear to relate to Tibetan Buddhism, the most common belief system in northwest China's provinces of Gansu and Qinghai. The area is home to several minorities in addition to Uyghurs and Tibetans, and was once considered part of Tibet.[32] It is unlikely the Kyoto carpets were from historical Tibet, since the carpet is not known to have become a serious medium for spiritual expression there.[33] The dyes, designs and structure of more recent carpets woven in Tibet bear no similarity to the

4.3

carpets in the Gion collections. With regard to the related ink-painted tapestries, tapestry weaving is not commonly practised in Tibet.

THE MONGOLS

As tent dwellers, the Mongols have traditionally had considerable demand for carpets. They were and still are used extensively for furnishing tents and dressing saddle horses. As ground covers just outside the tent door they extend the tent's living space. However, the Mongols themselves had little interest in carpet weaving, and traditionally preferred to obtain carpets from artisans discovered among their conquered peoples. During their many fierce conquests, the Mongols are said to have spared the lives of skilled weavers, as well as other expert craftsmen. These captives were then dispersed to workshops producing luxury goods for the Mongols. When the Mongol invaders arrived in northwest China under General Subutai in the thirteenth century, Uyghur men were taken as captives and the women were taken as mates. Weaving was a traditional male occupation in Uyghur society. It is possible that the Mongols commanded Uyghur men under their authority to create the carpets.

4.3

Painted Tapestry No. 85. Image of wrathful Tibetan deity. The portraits of Tibetan deities on Ink-painted tapestries Nos. 85, 86, and 87, led the investigation to the Tibetan Buddhist-populated regions of the Yellow River Corridor. Warp: 12 warps per 2.5 cm. Weft: 26 wefts per 2.5 cm. 158 x 108 cm. Courtesy Houka Boko Preservation Association.

51

4·4
The Teaching of
Manichaeism and Other
Narratives. *Hanging scroll
mounted as a panel, late
fourteenth century. 163.2 x
74.3 cm. Museum Yamato
Bunkakan, Nara. After Watt,
Khubilai Khan, 123.*

4·4

4.5

4.6

THE UYGHURS

Research repeatedly suggests that the ink-painted tapestries were in fact produced by Uyghurs, who are famed among textile historians for having practised and disseminated tapestry weaving in China.[34] The Uyghurs are particularly renowned for combining fine painting with tapestry weaving. The fact that the weavings are created in tapestry technique with finely painted details, outlines and accents, strongly points to the Uyghur people. New York's Metropolitan Museum of Art has published two voluminous, richly illustrated catalogues in recent years, each devoting several pages to the unique role the Uyghurs played in the production of tapestry over the centuries.[35] Although the museum catalogues focus on the silk tapestry so prized by the Chinese imperial family and the upper classes, references to wool tapestry appear as well. It is noted in the Metropolitan publications that silk and wool tapestry are created using the same technique. It is likely that the skilled weavers who wove tapestry produced fabric in both fibres, depending on the client and on the textile's function.

4.5
Detail, Painted Tapestry No.86. Image of Tibetan wrathful deity with 'net of jewels' and Curly Grass motifs. Courtesy Houka Boko Preservation Association.

4.6
Detail, Ink-Painted Tapestry No.65. This detail shows a typical drawing in black ink painted on the surface of the tapestries. The cloth is created by means of tapestry weave using single dovetailing. Extra eccentric wefts are inserted to create the curvilinear forms. Dyes of safflower red, now oxidized to brown and beige, appear along with indigo and natural white sheep's wool. Peacock and peony motifs appear on the background design of vertical segments of Light and Dark. Courtesy Minami Kannon Yama Preservation Association.

53

4·7

54

4·7
Diverse townspeople representing several minorities assemble at the outdoor vegetable market in the town of Chone in 2010. The minority Manichaeans were once denegrated by the majority Han Chinese as 'onion eaters.' 60 61

One of the first descriptions of tapestry weaving is in the *Songmo jiwen* (Records of the Pine Forests in the Plains), by Hong Hao (1088–1155). Hong Hao, an emissary of the Southern Song to the Jin court, was detained in Jin territory for fifteen years, primarily in the city of Yanjing, which eventually became Beijing. The *Songmo jiwen* tells of his long detention in the North, which provided him with an opportunity to observe the silk tapestry-woven robes worn by the Uyghurs in Beijing. He described them as 'resplendently beautiful'. Fragments of his original manuscript survive and were posthumously published by his son.36 The book provides a detailed account of the Uyghurs and their accomplishments in weaving tapestry.

In *When Silk Was Gold,* James Watt and Anne Wardwell describe Hong Hao's account of the history of the Uyghur refugees, who left their former empire in Mongolia, eventually resettling in Qinzhou, modern-day Tianshui. In addition to his documentation of the Uyghurs' striking tapestry-woven garments, Hong Hao also confirms that those Uyghurs who settled along the Gansu Corridor remained there,

4.8

4.9

even after the area was invaded by the Tanguts of the Xi Xia Kingdom in the early eleventh century.[37] Watt and Wardwell conclude that Uyghurs were the 'carriers of the technique of tapestry weaving'. They note that examples of tapestry may be found wherever Uyghurs settled.[38]

A monograph written by the late Jean Mailey, a highly esteemed textile curator at the Metropolitan Museum for some decades, also confirms the important role the Uyghurs played in developing tapestry.[39]

The footprints of the Uyghur artisans are revealed in the many Uyghur stylistic features on the Kyoto tapestries. These include the outlining of forms in black ink, a fondness for curvilinear motifs, a resistance to linear or rectangular shapes and right angles, indicating details by repeated parallel thin black lines,[40] and the abundant use of 'curly grass' motifs.

Although their bright colours have faded, it is likely that the painted tapestries were originally woven of yarn dyed in vibrant shades of red, blue, gold and green, as well as pink and turquoise, notable also in Uyghur murals and religious paintings. The brilliant multicoloured

4.8
Fruit is a mainstay of the Manichaean diet. Everywhere in the Monguor country, bushels of melons and grapes are conspicuously offered for sale at outdoor marketplaces.

4.9
Hui (Muslims), Tibetans, as well as Han Chinese and Monguor, shop at a marketplace in Minhe, Qinghai Province, northwest China.

56 4.10

Wall mural of mythical fish and animals swimming in the waves, a painting probably created by Uyghurs, at Luqu Shitshang Monastery, Gansu Province. A Uyghur wall painting at Bezeklik from the ninth to tenth centuries shows a similar treatment of sea monsters, waves and cone-shaped mountains.[62]

4.10

ink-painted tapestries uniformly appear on backgrounds dyed bright safflower red-orange. These vivid hues can also be observed over the centuries on depictions of Uyghur dress and architecture.

UYGHUR HISTORY, CULTURE AND DRESS

Zsuzsanna Gulácsi has admirably described Manichaean textiles and costumes from this region based on her studies of recovered Manichaean codices and illuminated manuscripts produced through the eleventh century.[41] In a second volume she describes the dress of the Manichaean 'elect'. She states that the wearing of full-length white robes by elects is essential to identifying a society as Manichaean.[42]

However, there are no white robes, nor any fragments of white robes, stored in the material in Kyoto. The ink-painted tapestries and the pile carpets alone represent the many shipments of the textiles that arrived in Japan over a 350-year period. Their many Manichaean motifs and designs must be explained despite the absence of white robes. One may presume that robes made of white cotton or linen may have deteriorated and been discarded more rapidly than mantles woven of wool. It is also possible that plain garments of linen or cotton were of little use in the cold mountainous regions of Gansu-Qinghai, so they were discarded.

On the northwest Chinese ink-painted tapestries, images of eyes are ubiquitous. They appear singly, floating around other images, as features of the many birds portrayed, and on the cranes that replace the peacock images. Almond-shaped eyes with a dot for the pupil appear on the bodhisattvas illustrated on the tenth- and eleventh-century banners; interestingly they appear again as the crane's eyes on the southern coastal painted tapestries woven from the sixteenth to twentieth centuries. The almond-shaped eye with dot for pupil represents bird's eyes on the painted and printed tapestries woven in Jiangsu and Zhejiang provinces.[43]

In the Turfan region in the tenth century, aggressive neighbours forced the far western group of Uyghur migrants to abandon their Manichaean and Buddhist beliefs and adopt Islam, practised in the Xinjiang region to the present day. However, there is no evidence of Islamic features on any of the carpets or painted tapestries in Kyoto. The Uyghurs who migrated eastward to Gansu-Qinghai in the ninth century remained Manichaean, along with their descendants. Eventually they absorbed Tibetan Buddhism and Taoism as well,[44] while avoiding the conversion to Islam.

Uyghur clans that were originally determined to remain Manichaean established colonies along the Yellow River and its tributaries in the provinces of Qinghai and Gansu.[45] With time the influence of their Tibetan hosts in the region became overwhelming and many adopted Tibetan Buddhist beliefs. Tibetan Buddhism, some remnants of their early Shamanism, along with elements of Taoism, continue to be the faiths professed outwardly by most of the population to the present day.

The Chinese government has committed to religious freedom and has seemingly determined that keeping peace in the region is preferable to condemning a religion outright. It has given some high-placed (Tibetan Buddhist) lamas official Chinese titles and positions. My experience travelling in the region was that the old Manichaean beliefs have not been entirely extinguished. Some families appear to quietly practise both sets of beliefs and Taoism as well, a syncretism not uncommon in Asia.

The Chinese frequently revile the Uyghurs who settled in Xinjiang in the far west of China for their supposedly bellicose

58

4.11

4.12

nature. As long ago as the Tang Dynasty the Uyghurs were referred to as 'tyrannical and proud'.[46] At present the Muslim Uyghurs of Xinjiang are accused of 'separatism' and worse. It is difficult to get Chinese scholars to talk about Uyghur artistic contributions. It is a moot point, as the Uyghur artwork of Xinjiang bears no similarity to the textiles and carpets under discussion. These artworks were created by Uyghurs who practised Manichaeanism and Tibetan Buddhism. There are no Islamic features or influences on any of the carpets or ink-painted tapestries in Kyoto.

During the last decade of the twentieth century and the first decade of the twenty-first I travelled to China to investigate the origins of the carpets and tapestries. Research trips were made in 1995, 1998, 2004, 2005, 2006, 2007 and 2010. Although I focused on Gansu and Qinghai provinces, Ningxia province was also explored. My quest was to locate the descendants of the several Uyghur Manichaean clans who had migrated to Gansu and Qinghai provinces (united as a single province of Gansu in 1928) from the ninth century on.[47] It appeared that the

4.13

Uyghur Manichaean weavers and painters
had become meshed with other minorities,
taken different names, or had dissolved into
the Han Chinese majority. The Manichaean
religion had been repeatedly reviled and
intermittently outlawed in China over the
centuries.[48] It was hard to explain therefore
the textiles with Manichaean designs that
continued to enter the Associations' vaults
through the mid nineteenth century. Artists
and weavers were designing and producing
them and someone was ordering and/or
paying for them. Not finding the answers, I
hypothesised that the Manichaean designs
might also appear on other art forms in the
region, perhaps on items less fragile than
textiles. The traces of unique spiritual
beliefs dear to tens of thousands of Uyghur
immigrants might still be evident if one
searched thoroughly.

Visits were made to monasteries,
marketplaces, weaving workshops,
universities and museums in the search for
traces of Manichaean culture. Today,
surviving and renamed Buddhist
monasteries are in remote and near
inaccessible locations, no doubt offering
the few worshippers some sense of security.

4.13
*Migration of the Uyghurs in
the 840s. Immigrants also
travelled northeast, establishing
settlements in Qinzhou
(Tianshui) and Beijing.
Map after Takao Moriyasu,
World History
Reconsidered through
the Silk Road, Osaka
University Twenty-First-
Century COE Program,
Interface Humanities Research
Activities 2002/2003,
Osaka, Japan: Osaka
University, 2002, 331,
map 7.*

4.14

4.14
Map of Xining Garrison. In this map, dating from the early Ming Dynasty, the round tents of the Monguors can be discerned. The individuals wearing red garments are probably Monguors as well. In the beginning of their stay in Gansu, it is likely they carefully maintained the Turkic preference for red and robed themselves in that colour. For the Uyghurs red is the colour of blood, thus it represents 'Life'. Chinese conscripts had recently arrived in Xining but no Chinese buildings are yet visible on this map. The Chinese called the Monguors they encountered 'Tu', meaning 'aboriginals' or 'natives', assuming incorrectly that they had always inhabited the region. Today Xining is the capital of Qinghai Province. Courtesy Charles E. Young Research Library Map Collection, University of California at Los Angeles.

60

The multiple murals and thangkas that decorate monastery walls are expressive of Tibetan Buddhism. Therefore it was heartening to discover the mandala on the wall of Luqu Shitshang monastery. It portrayed miniatures encircling Mount Meru in much the same style as some pictured on examples preserved in Kyoto (Nos. 90–93). The mural also resembles a silk tapestry (*kesi*) mandala dated to the Yuan dynasty (1279–1368 CE) in the collection of the Metropolitan Museum in New York,[49] very probably the work of Uyghur artists.

MIGRATION TO GANSU-QINGHAI
Several scholars have described the settlements established by the Uyghurs east of Turfan in Gansu province. Drompp describes the diaspora of the Uyghurs following their defeat by the Kyrgyz in the eighth century. He describes the settlements in Turfan and also those in the Yellow River corridor of Gansu.[50] Moriyasu concurs, referring to Chinese sources that discuss the fate of the Uyghurs after the defeat of their East Uyghur Khanate in 840 CE. Moriyasu explains that there were three groups of Uyghurs that migrated westward: the largest

4.15

4.16

group went to the eastern part of the Tian Shan region; another group went to the environs of Ganzhou (now Zhangye) in the Gansu corridor; and the third group went to the Semirechye region on the north side of the western part of the Tian Shan mountain range.[51]

Ghang Lian Ji traces the arrival of Uyghur tribes in Gansu and Qinghai after crossing the Qilian Shan Mountains during the Tang dynasty, and their resettlement in the Xining region.[52]

Watt and Wardwell describe how Qinzhou (presently Tianshui), Gansu province, became home to a colony of Uyghur tapestry weavers in the ninth century. By the tenth to twelfth centuries the neighbouring Xi Xia (Tangut people), seeking to wrest control of the profitable Silk Route from the Uyghurs headquartered in their capital of Ganzhou (Zhangye), conquered part of that territory. In the tenth century, fleeing the Xi Xia aggression, some tribes accepted the invitation to settle offered by the powerful Tibetan chieftain Chü-eh-szu-lo (997–1065), governor of Xining, capital of Gansu-Qinghai.[53] Yang Fuxue describes Uyghur migrations to the

4.15
The outskirts of Xining, lined with red hills, on approach to the city from the north. (2010).

4.16
A weaver at recess, wool-weaving workshop, Qinzhou, 2010.

61

4.17

4.17
Reeling wool yarn at the factory in Qinzhou, 2010.

Beijing area and other towns in inner China during the Yuan Dynasty (1279–1378 CE).[55] He also explains that, after the Uyghur kingdom collapsed, some Uyghurs stayed on in their former capital of Ganzhou, but many fled both east and west.

UYGHURS IN XINING

It is recorded that, among the Uyghurs who settled in Xining, the Uyghur Dongxi Tusi became a *Youcheng* (provincial official) in the Yuan Dynasty.[55] In 1371, having submitted to the Ming, he was appointed a Director for the city of Xining. Over the next several

hundred years to 1931 his descendants, occupying the office of Donxi Tusi, governed several towns and villages in the environs of the cities of Xining, Minhe and Ledu, originally encompassing more than 3,000 residents and 100 soldiers.[56]

Chü-eh-szu-lo's territory was a multi-ethnic political regime, within which Tibetans were the majority. When the Xi Xia (Tanguts) seized the Gansu corridor, they made unreasonable demands on merchants passing through that territory, forcing trade caravans that came and went between the (far) western regions (today's

4.18

4.19

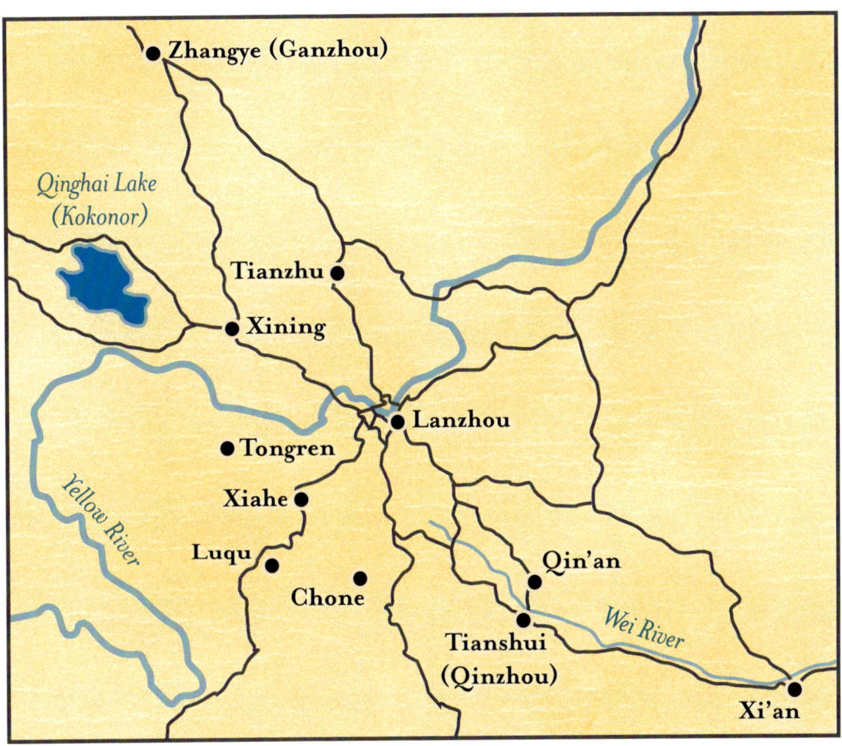

4.20

Xinjiang) and China's central plains to pay what the traders felt were exorbitant duties. This practice resulted in many caravans making a detour south through Xining. Chü-eh-szu-lo welcomed the caravans, rightly perceiving this as an opportunity to augment Xining's international trade. Successive rulers of Chü-eh-szu-lo's territory continued to take advantage of the caravans' detour, further augmenting Xining's economy and strengthening defences. Xining was then and is now a bustling marketplace, and is also considered the gateway to Tibet.

UYGHURS IN QINZHOU (TIANSHUI)

The Uighurs became 'naturalised' Chinese citizens. When the Jin Jurchens took over the area, many Uighurs were moved north to the vicinity of Yanjing (present-day Beijing), but apparently some of them stubbornly stayed on in the Qinzhou area. Hong Hao praised the great beauty of their textiles, costumes and tapestry-woven mandalas.[57]

It may seem unreasonable to assume that, after so many centuries, tapestry is still being woven in Qinzhou. In fact the town – now just a district in Tianshui City – is today producing wool carpets and a type of wool

4.18

Many tapestries woven in Qinzhou today use pile carpet-weaving 'tapestry' techniques to depict the Potala Palace in Lhasa. The tapestries are exported to Lhasa for sale to pilgrims and tourists.

4.19

Wool-weaving workshop in Qinzhou, 2010.

4.20

Map of Uyghur population centres with access to Yellow River waterways.

63

tapestry. The workshops I visited there in 2010 were actively weaving wool tapestries by means of a faster and less demanding technique than would have been required to produce the ink-painted tapestries preserved in Kyoto. I did not see any tapestries that utilise classic tapestry technique being currently produced.[58]

Although Qinzhou gained fame as a centre of silk tapestry production, reportedly wool has always been woven there as well. Tapestry, whether silk or wool, is created using the same technique. It is reasonable to hypothesise that the workshops in Qinzhou, documented as producing tapestry in China for 500 years before ink-painted tapestries began arriving in Japan, may have served as the site of manufacture for the ink-painted tapestries that wound up secured in the Kyoto lockers.

My trip to Qinzhou and its remaining wool-weaving production centres was fruitful – with one glitch. I toured the factory and attempted to interview an elderly weaver who did not appear to be Han Chinese. As our conversation began, a female majordomo of imposing stature blocked my way and brusquely sent the elderly weaver packing into the depths of the factory. Later, as I was leaving the building, I noted that, across the upper façade, above the entryway, a large luxuriantly feathered bird had been elaborately painted long ago. Though dimmed, it was still possible to make out the image of the multicoloured peacock, talismanic bird of the Manichaeans!

During the Yuan and Ming Dynasties, Uyghur population centres were bustling wool markets with access to Yellow River waterways, the main means of transportation. Today the towns of Lanzhou, Qinzhou (Tianshui), Qin'an and Chone are all within a two-hour drive of one another. ❧

NOTES

31. According to Prof. Pamela Crossley, Dartmouth College, the vibrant hues of blue, yellow, purple, green and vermillion, often seen on Korean costume, were also probably bestowed by the Uyghurs. These are certainly distinct from the surrounding colour preferences in East Asia. Personal communication, May 22, 1995.

32. Gyurme Dorje, *Footprint Tibet* (Chicago: Passport Books, 1996), 604–9, 685–91. After some confusing episodes I learned that all residents were referred to as 'Tibetans' by the surrounding Chinese and sometimes by themselves.

33. Murray L. Eiland, *Chinese and Exotic Rugs* (Boston: New York Graphic Society, 1979), 102–05.

34. Some authorities believe that the Uyghurs learned tapestry weaving from the Sogdians. See Watt, James C.Y. and Anne E. Wardwell. *When Silk Was Gold: Central Asian and Chinese Textiles* (New York: Metropolitan Museum of Art, 1997).

35. Watt, James C.Y., *The World of Khubilai Khan: Chinese Art in the Yuan Dynasty.* (New York: Metropolitan Museum of Art, 2010).

36. Watt and Wardwell explain that the character for Qinzhou is misprinted in some modern texts, but insist that the city of Qinzhou is what was meant in the original text. See *When Silk Was Gold,* 63, n.27.

37. Watt and Wardwell. *When Silk Was Gold,* 62.

38. Watt and Wardwell, *When Silk Was Gold,* 61–62.

39. Jean Mailey, *Chinese Silk Tapestry: K'o-ssu* (New York: The China Institute in America 1971), 10–11.

40. Russell-Smith, *Uygur Patronage,* 237. For a table illustrating the key features that identify Uyghur influence, see pages III, 114.

41. Zsuzsanna Gulácsi, *Manichaean Art in Berlin Collections,* Corpus Fontium Manichaeorum: Series Archaeologica et Iconographica (Belgium: Brepols, 2001); *Mediaeval Manichaean Book Art: A Codicological Study of Iranian and Turkic Illuminated Book Fragments from Eighth to Eleventh Century East Central Asia,* Nag Hammadi and Manichaean Studies 57 (Leiden: Brill, 2005), 25.

42. Gulácsi 2005: 25.

43. Bhattacharya-Haesner. 2003. Figure 154.1, 68, Figure 553. 60, Figure 291.

44. The border motif, erroneously labelled Kufic in some publications, is actually based on old Turkic runiform lettering. See Fig. 3.21a-c.

45. Michael R. Drompp, *Tang China and the Collapse of the Uighur Empire: A Documentary ,* Leiden: Brill's Inner Asian Library 13 (Leiden: Brill, 2005) 197.

46. Drompp, *Tang China,* 283.

47. Louis M. J. Schram, *The Monguors of the Kansu– Tibetan Frontier, Records of the Monguor Clans: History of the Monguors in Huangchung and the Chronicles of the Lu Family,* Transactions of the American Philosophical Society 47 (Philadelphia: American Philosophical Society, 1961), Vol 51 Pt 3, Preface I, 14–23, 30.

48. Louis M.J. Schram, *The Monguors of the Kansu-Tibetan Frontier,* Vol.44 Pt.1; Samuel N.C. Lieu, *Manichaeism in Central Asia and China,* Nag Hammadi and Manichaean Studies 45, (Boston: Brill, 1998), 153–55.

49. Watt, *The World of Khubilai Khan,* Figure 262. Cosmological Mandala with Mount Meru. Silk tapestry.

50. Drompp, *Tang China,* 197.

51. Takao Moriyasu. 'The Flourishing of Manichaeism under the West Uighur Kingdom. New Edition of the Uighur Charter on the Administration of the Manichaean Monastery in Qoco.' In *World History Reconsidered through the Silk Road.* Osaka University Twenty-First Century COE Program, Interface Humanities Research Activities 2002/2003. (Osaka, Japan: Osaka University, 2003), 93.

52. Ji, Ghang Lian. *Si lu, zou lang de bao gao: Gan Qing te you min zu wen hua xing tai yan jiu* [Researches on the Cultural Formation of the Ethnic Groups Which Live Only in Gansu and Qinghai]. Beijing: Min zu chu ban she, 1999.

53. R.A. Stein, *Tibetan Civilization,* (Stanford: Stanford University Press, 1972), 71.

54. Fuxue Yang, 'Where Did the Ganzhou Uighurs Go After the Kingdom Collapsed?' *A Summary of the Research of History of Northwest Minorities, Dunhuang Studies,* The Almanac of Research of Minority History in China. (Beijing: Minzu Press, 1994), 212.

55. *Tusi* means 'clan leader,' a position established at the beginning of the Ming Dynasty and continuing to 1931. Keith W. Slater, *A Grammar of Mangghuer: A Mongolic Language of China's Qinghai-Gansu Sprachbund* (London: Routledge, 2003), 17.

56. Zhengde Yan and Yiwu Wang, ed., *Qinghai Encyclopedic Dictionary,* Zinghai Baike Dacidian (Beijing: China Financial and Economic Press, 1994).

57. Denny, Joyce, in Watt and Wardwell (2010) 243, 246.

58. I did observe silk tapestry weavers still actively producing luxury goods in Nanjing and also viewed examples at the National Silk Museum, Hangzhou. Traditional Chinese auspicious motifs and designs were the topics of these weavings.

59. Drompp, *Tang China,* 197–98.

60. Lieu, *Manichaeism in Central Asia and China,* 153–55.

61. Watt, *The World of Khubilai Khan.* Figure 262.

62. Mario Bussagli, *Central Asian Painting, Treasures of Asia* (New York: Rizzoli, 1979), 109.

63. Watt and Wardwell. *When Silk Was Gold,* 101-03.

5

INK-PAINTED TAPESTRIES IN CHINA

In July 1998 I left the solemn monasteries and quiet towns nestled in the mountains of the Monguor country and travelled to Lanzhou, the lively provincial capital, to view the collections of the Gansu Provincial Museum. There, across a spacious conference chamber, I spied the edge of what appeared to be an ink-painted tapestry. The adept museum staff, working from the photos of the Kyoto collections that I had sent ahead, had figured out which objects in their collection related to the focus of my research.

I stared at the folded textile before me and approached hesitantly, not quite believing my eyes. The staff members witnessed my struggle to control my excitement. Trembling, I was given permission to touch the tapestry.

The red-orange wool was incredibly thick and soft, resembling the costly double-knit cashmere sold in western department stores and typical of the sheep's wool described as that produced in Gansu-Qinghai provinces.[64] In its fibre, dyes, weaving technique and subject matter, the example before

5.1
Detail of Ink-Painted Tapestry No.91, Fig.5.4. Taoist themes fill the central octagon. Courtesy Tsuki Boko Preservation Association.

5.2

5.2

*Ink-Painted Tapestry No.89.
The Light and Dark segments
have become reduced to broad
and narrow stripes at each end.
The once-prominent peonies
seem to be transmigrating to
caterpillars and butterflies.
Wood-block printed leafy sprays,
a style originating during the
Liao Dynasty, cover the background and the ground of the
central fan motif. Warp: 10 warps
per 2.5 cm. Weft: 40 wefts per
2.5 cm. Early Ming Dynasty.
176 x 122 cm. Courtesy Kanko
Boko Preservation Association.*

me appeared near identical to the weavings
in Kyoto.

The Gansu Provincial Museum's early
examples reveal the same superior wool
fibre, the same red-orange safflower dye,
the same tapestry woven with inserted
eccentric wefts, as seen in Kyoto.
Disappointingly the members of the staff
have absolutely no information regarding
their fine collection of ink-painted
tapestries. It was mysteriously declared
that no one knew anything about the
identity of the artisans, precisely where in
Gansu the weavings were woven, or what

purpose they had originally served.
Nevertheless, it was undeniable that since
acquisition they had been officially housed
and maintained in the institution
dedicated to the preservation of the
artworks of Gansu province.[65]

It was during this visit that the ink-
painted tapestries in the Gansu Provincial
Museum's collection were dated by then vice
director Zhang Pengchuan as 'early Ming'
(1368–1435 CE). He believed that they were
of local production. He told me that they
had been discovered in a temple storeroom
in the town of Qin'an, around 250

5·3

kilometres east of Lanzhou. The tapestries had come into the museum collection in the years just after the Cultural Revolution (1966–1976 CE). On a subsequent visit Prof. Zhang, by then a doctoral tutor at the School of Arts, Suzhou University, Jiangsu province, offered the opinion that the ink-painted tapestries in Kyoto were very likely woven in or around Qin'an, and stated outright his belief that in recent centuries Japanese buyers had custom-ordered ink-painted tapestries in Jiangsu on the south eastern Chinese coast and had them shipped to Japan.

The earlier ink-painted tapestries first appear in Japanese sketches of the Gion Festival in the late 1400s CE and appear in screen paintings by the early 1500s CE. In Kyoto, scholars estimate that artworks produced abroad during the Muromachi Period (1333–1373 CE) through to the Edo Period (1600–1868 CE) might have taken anything from one to 100 years to get to Kyoto.

On a later visit to the Gansu Provincial Museum, a few more examples of the ink-painted tapestries were located and brought out of storage [5.3]. These appear

5·3
Ink-painted tapestry, middle Ming Dynasty. A pen and black ink were used to enhance the tapestry-woven figures resembling the Taoist sages. In the background, undulating mountain formations alternate with wavy foliage, and curving tree trunks with leafy clusters. 85 cm x 170 cm. Collection, Gansu Provincial Museum, Lanzhou.

70

5·4

to have been woven a few decades later. Figures resembling the Taoist sages had almost entirely replaced the earlier Manichaean and Buddhist motifs. The topics portrayed on the later ink-painted tapestries in the Gansu Provincial Museum Collection resemble the later Kyoto examples, those with increasing Buddhist and Taoist themes.

In Lanzhou in 2010 I also met the esteemed Prof. Chen Bingying, executive editor of the text *Chinese Minority Peoples and the History of Scientific Technology*,[66] who, sympathetic to my plight, explained that the tapestry workshops were actually located east of Qin'an in the town of Zhang Jya Chuan (Zhang Family Valley). They were taken to the larger market town of Qin'an to be sold. Prof. Chen also told me that Qi'nan was once home to a large population of 'Central Asians'.[67] It seems that in China the term 'Central Asians' is considered a polite appellation for Uyghur people.

Professors Zhang and Chen having explained that the Qin'an region was heavily populated by 'Central Asians' during the Yuan Dynasty, I pondered whether the grand Xingguo temple in that city might have originally been a Uyghur Manichaean institution. The main hall had exposed interior beams, a characteristic of Manichaean temple architecture.[68] It was undeniable that the temple had become a Buddhist temple in a later incarnation and its current designation is that of a National Historical Museum.

During the fourteenth century wood-block printing began to replace the pen and black ink drawings on the ink-painted tapestries. A few details, possibly those deemed especially meaningful, continued to receive the fine painter's attention. The evolution to wood-block printing is somewhat surprising as the Manichaeans particularly treasured their proficiency in fine painting along with their mastery of the arts of calligraphy.[69] The Manichaeans were also accomplished sculptors, as revealed by their skilfully carved woodblocks as well as by their statuary. The blocks facilitated expanded production of their abundant illuminated literature. Sculpting carved woodblocks and printing with them became a serious focus of monastic endeavours for centuries at Chone monastery. Not far from the looms at Qinzhou and trading centre at Qin'an, it became particularly renowned for illuminated copies of the Buddhist sutras.[70] One wonders whether the same dedicated monks who produced the illuminated Manichaean texts and Buddhist sutras also block-printed the floral backgrounds of the later ink-painted tapestries.

CHONE, THE TECHNICOLOR TEMPLE

Chone Monastery (*Chanding si*. Chinese), serenely nestled in a valley beside a bend in the Tao River, is particularly famed for the production of expertly carved wood blocks. The blocks may originally have been carved to print Manichaean literature but, after the fifteenth century, they were probably produced to print Buddhist sutras.

Chone Monastery also became known for the cultivation of rare and unusual peonies.[71] The latter became particularly celebrated thanks to the botanist Joseph Rock, who lived at Chone Monastery for nearly two years in the early twentieth century. A peony with luminescent white petals and a maroon splotch is named for him, *peony rockii*. Rock was introduced to the intriguingly hued flower by a monk around 1912.

It seems the area continued to be home to a few remaining Manichaean devotees. The cultivators of the unusual peony may well have striven to represent light and dark themes. As the author Annemarie von Gabain documented so well, it was a

5.4

Ink-Painted Tapestry No. 91. The orientation has changed to a vertical format, possibly related to a new function. Taoist themes fill the central octagon. In the background, woodblock printing surrounds surviving hand-painted images. Warp: 12 warps per 2.5 cm. Weft: 29 wefts per 2.5 cm. 163 x 124 cm. Courtesy Tsuki Boko Preservation Association.

72 5·5

*Ink-Painted Tapestry
No.66. Peacock, magpie
and peony appear. The
fractured image of a peacock
is seen on a ground of
Light and Dark segments
amid Curly Grass motifs.
Fractured images are a
consistent feature of the
ink-painted tapestries.
Courtesy Naginata Boko
Preservation Association.*

5·5

5.6

Manichaean practice to utilise objects in nature that exhibited characteristics of light and dark as well as to create utilitarian objects similarly decorated.[72]

On my first attempt to reach Chone Monastery in October 2007 I was turned back by icy mountain roads. However, I managed to arrive there safely in late summer 2010. The satisfaction I felt on reaching the site gave me the optimistic feeling that Chone Monastery might finally solve some of the enigmas that continued to perplex me. The monastery, ruled for centuries by the family and descendants of a Tibetan *t'u-ssu* (clan headman) as an independent principality, was filled everywhere with impressive murals and painted sculptures.[73] The astonishing artwork suggested that the monastery and its surroundings might have played a role in providing a haven for surviving Manichaean artists. The religion was particularly harshly repressed by the third reign of the Ming dynasty (1403–1424 CE) and its many practitioners were dispersed.

The unique independent political status of Chone (only relinquished in 1928), as

5.6

Leafy sprays (possibly fragrant eucalyptus leaves) framed by a highlighted green border, are painted on the overhead beams of the entryway at Chone Temple. They strongly resemble the leaves block-printed on Ink-Painted Tapestries Nos. 88–92, preserved in Kyoto. A variety of leaves and branches appear throughout the images on the ink-painted tapestries, seen on those preserved in China, and also appearing on those preserved in Japan.

5.7

5.8

74

5.7
At dusk, branches are carried by acolyte monks to the evening ritual of creating fragrant smoke. Upper Wutun Temple, Gansu Province.

5.8
Exposed ceiling beams, Xingguo Temple, Qin'an, Gansu Province. It was a Manichaean tradition that ceiling beams remained unpainted.

well as its fairly inaccessible location, may have recommended it as a refuge to migrant painters and sculptors seeking relief from persecution. It may have seemed an inviting place where artists could safely continue practising their profession.

At the entrance to the nearly silent and today mostly abandoned monastery complex sits a building in the style of a Chinese Pavilion. The structure and its façade exude an aura of sanctity, having welcomed multitudes of worshippers over centuries of sacramental rites. Elaborately carved and painted birds and brilliant blossoms stun

the viewer with the cunning of their forms and the surviving vibrancy of their hues. Some, protected by the roof overhang, are sparklingly fresh in colour despite hundreds of years of exposure to the elements. Above the entrance, carved and painted peacocks hover, protecting all who enter from harm [9.51].

The entire building is elaborately chiselled and coated with bright paint. Lintels, struts and joists painstakingly depict the symbols cherished by the pious Manichaean artisans. The structure reflects centuries of efforts by talented sculptor and painter devotees. The back of the building, away from direct sunlight, reveals colours still sharp and bold. On crossbeams, painted leafy decorations resembling in style those that appear on the later painted tapestries in Kyoto greet the visitor. Among them, multiple clusters of grey-green oval-shaped leaves suggest the odoriferous eucalyptus. The images of vegetation are grazed, and were too high above the ground for me to make positive identification. However, a little lower (and more startling as one looks up between the rafters high in the air), a panoply of brightly coloured and realistically portrayed ripe vegetables present themselves (see Chapter 6, Vegetarianism). Here I viewed sculpted and painted images of radishes, turnips, carrots and leafy greens in faithful rendition [6.10]. I had arrived!

NOTES

64. Charles I. Rostov and Jia Guanyan, *Chinese Carpets* (New York: Harry N. Abrams, 1983): 73, pl 110.

65. The Cultural Revolution (1966–1976) had made museum scholarship near impossible to pursue for that decade and it has yet to recover.

66. Bingying Chen, *Zhongguo shaoshu minzu ke Xue Ji Shushi Congshu* [Chinese minority peoples and the history of scientific technology] (Nanning, China: Guangxi Kexue Jishu Chubanshe, 1996).

67. Bingying Chen, personal communication, 2005. Lanzhou, Gansu, China.

68. Cultural China website, 'Beams inside the Manichaean Hall,' http://history.cultural-china.com/en/164H3736H10340.html, accessed May 7, 2013.

69. Klimkeit 1982. 20.

70. One set of carved blocks from Chone Monastery, though damaged, is said to be preserved in the United States Library of Congress Collection.

71. Andreas Gruschke, *The Cultural Monuments of Tibet's Outer Provinces: Amdo*, vol. 1, *The Qinghai Part of Amdo* (Bangkok: White Lotus, 2001), 17; also Grushke vol. 2, 44–46.

72. Annemarie von Gabain, *Das Leben im uigurischen Königreich von Qočo: 850–1250* (Weisbaden, Germany: Harrassowitz, 1973), fig. 14, fig. 56.

73. The role of *t'u-ssu* is described in Slater p. 17.

6

MANI AND THE RELIGION OF LIGHT

Manichaeanism was founded in the third century by Mani, born in 215–16 CE to a family distantly related to the Persian nobility, in what is today Iraq. The name Mani is thought to connote 'the illustrious' and is a title and term of respect rather than a proper name. This title, assumed by the founder, completely replaced his personal name. Mani created a holy book called the *Arzhang* that colourfully illustrated the tenets of his faith. He became known as 'The Painter' – and to the present day that is the basis for his fame in Iran. His followers developed painting skills and carried and displayed their canvases in foreign lands to spread the word of Mani. Manichaean missionaries carried picture books with them, allowing them to communicate with the mostly illiterate populace they encountered. Mani also produced a body of literature to serve those followers who were literate.

PRINCIPLES OF MANICHAEANISM

The belief in a duality consisting of the forces of light in a constant struggle with the powers of darkness is the essence of the religion. The worship and protection of light

6.2

Mani is portrayed in a tall hat covered with vegetal motifs. Identified as 'curly vine or floral motifs' by Gulácsi. The hat is secured on a tripodal base. After Bussagli, Central Asian Painting, *105.*

6.3

The bold Curly Grass motifs at the top left of this temple building are a motif usually found wherever Manichaean institutions survive. This is Rongbo Gonchen in the town of Tongren. It was established in 1301 CE, probably as a Manichaean Temple. It became the site of a Tibetan Buddhist monastery.

6.4

Panel for upper garment worn by Monguors, twentieth century. Outlining and multiple outlining embroidery techniques. Some images appear three dimensional as well. The careful juxtaposition of the dark ground and bright embroidery threads enable the designs to appear to glow. The yin yang symbol in the centre of the panel reveals the absorption of Taoist ideas among the Monguour.[96]

6.2

6.3

78

is a central theme of Mani's philosophy. Manichaean artworks often appear to glow or to reflect light. This characteristic may be observed on temple wall murals, sculpture and carvings, as well as on the costumes of the Uyghurs' descendants, the Monguor.

According to Mani, light and good emanate from the spiritual universe and darkness and evil from the realm of the material world, including the human body, its appetites, and functions. The Realm of Light ('Good') was originally separated from the Realm of Darkness ('Evil') but, during a continuous struggle, dark overcame light and

the two essences became mixed. The two contiguous realms exist side by side. The present state of the universe represents a mixture of light and darkness as dark swallows up light. It is the duty of the Manichaean to release this light and protect it from any activity that might damage it.[74] It is through pursuit of redeeming knowledge that light conquers dark.[75] The opposing realms are also incorporated into two distinct beings. In the Realm of Light the Father of Greatness dwells. Evil spirits emanate from the Realm of Darkness, controlled by the Ruler of the Dark.[76]

6.4

6.5

On the ink-painted tapestries, Manichaean theology is expressed with repetitions of images depicting the struggle between light and dark. The paintings also portray awakened light liberated from darkness. Converts are guaranteed salvation if they can perpetuate this repetition and convert another individual in turn.[77]

EMBRACING CHRISTIANITY

By the third century, when Mani was building his following, Christianity was gaining in popularity in the Middle East. Wishing his religion to be all-inclusive, Mani integrated Christian themes. The idea of Christ, particularly the events surrounding the Passion, was interpreted as the sufferings of Light combating Dark. Mani declared himself an apostle of Christ (though the life of Jesus preceded that of Mani by three centuries), but he rejected certain aspects of the biblical account of the historic Jesus. For example, Mani felt it impossible that a divine entity could be killed. A version of Jesus called 'Jesus the Splendour' became a part of Manichaean worship. Manichaean hymns expressed confidence in the redemptive powers of Jesus.[78]

6.5

An embroidered Monguor costume panel, stitched to produce the effect of glowing peony blossoms, c. 1950. The corner elements of each embroidered square may also be noted in the designs of the audience carpets created exclusively for the use of Monguor's Living Buddhas.[97]

6.6

6.6

Glowing Monguor embroidered bib. Twentieth century. Monguor women perfected the use of embroidery techniques that enabled their motifs to appear to glow with their absorbed light. Fowler Museum at UCLA, X2013.52.23.

CAPTURING THE LIGHT

The monastery of Rongpo Gonchen in Gansu [9.21] was established during the Yuan Dynasty in 1301 CE.[79] A Manichaean cross appears on the temple below 'curly grass' and spiral motifs [7.24]. The highlighted bars of the cross resemble modern neon lighting. The glow has been achieved by means of specific painting techniques often employed by Manichaean artists in embellishing their religious institutions. Manichaean textiles also appear to glow and to reflect light. This feature may still be observed, accomplished by means of

embroidery techniques, on the costumes worn by the Uyghurs' descendants, the minority Chinese group called the Monguor (or 'Tu' by the Chinese). A thirteenth-century relief sculpture of Mani uncovered in Quanzhou, Fujian province, has been described by Prof. Samuel Lieu as 'skillfully carved, the carver using stones of different hues to achieve a luminous effect' [6.7].[80]

Gilded temple columns survive on some former Manichaean temples in Northwest China. It is documented that the Uyghurs greatly enjoyed gold decoration, and applied it wherever feasible. It is likely that when

6.7

6.8

they became Manichaeans in the eighth century, the metal's unique ability to reflect light increased the Uyghurs' affection for it.

VEGETARIANISM AND ASCETICISM

Vegetarianism is a core principle for Manichaeans. The devout believe that plants have souls and should be protected until tenderly harvested and ritually consumed.[81] Vegetables, fruits and plants are perceived as sacred receptacles of light and are the main source of sustenance for Manichaeans. Manichaean meeting places were called 'vegetarian halls'.[82] The consumption of

vegetables and fruits was believed to increase the light particles in the body. Meals are sacred events that set light particles free from the food containing them.[83] When believers eat and digest vegetables, the light contained within them is ingested in the body and then passed on to nature, in a sort of spiritual transformation, released through prayer and meditation.[84] Animals, though, are components of matter; their meat, as well as animal-like behaviour, is considered repellent and is rejected.

Members were required to lead an ascetic lifestyle. Stringent demands included

6.7

Painted relief sculpture of Mani, c. 1339, by Chen Xhenze, Cao'an Temple, Fujian. It seems that the sculptor carefully selected a variety of stones in an effort to capture the reflection of Light. After Lin Wu-shu, Mo ni jiao ji qi dong jian [Manichaeism and its eastward expansion], Taipei, Taiwan: Shu Xin, 1997.

6.8

Gilded column, Rongbo Temple, Tongren, Gansu Province, northwest China.

82   6.9

*Ink–Painted Tapestry No.83.
Fortuitous peony blossoms
surround Light and Dark
guardian dog pairs with triple
Curly Grass motif tails. In this
late example, only one dog
remains, standing guard in the
centre. Sturdy peony stalks form
gracious sentinels on the end
panels. Warp: 9 warps per 2.5
cm. Weft: 32 wefts per 2.5 cm.
158 x 84 cm. Courtesy Houka
Boko Preservation Association.*

6.9

refraining from meat, wine and sexual intercourse. Since not everyone could uphold such strict standards, there were two levels of worshippers: the 'elect', who met all the obligations; and the 'hearers', who cultivated food, collected alms, and served the elect. Their participation freed the elect from the need to interact with the material world.[85]

The most important religious expressions of Manichaeanism were regular prayers, services, scheduled fasts, and feast days. Seven two-day fasts were held during the year and otherwise meals were limited to one a day.[86] Hymns and worship took place every day, in private homes and temples.

SPREADING THE FAITH

Mani travelled extensively, making trips to India, Persia and Tibet, to win followers and to refine his philosophical ideas.[87] These ultimately won favour with the ruler of Persia, where he settled. Mani wished his religion to be universal and all embracing. He set up an extensive missionary programme and encouraged followers of other faiths to join him, gaining converts among Persian Zoroastrians, Egyptian Christians and Indian Buddhists. In doing so, however, he alienated many in the targeted communities. In his adopted Persia, his influential royal sponsor passed away and a ruler antagonistic to Mani came to power. Mani was attacked and imprisoned, leading to his premature death in 276 CE.

Nevertheless, centuries later, in 762 CE in Luoyang, China, a momentous event took place. A mission composed of Mani's devoted followers managed to convert the ruler of the Uyghurs, then in control of northern China.[88] After their conversion, centres of the Manichaean religion were established in Uyghur communities to the west in the Turfan region, in Beshbalik, in Qočo, in Dunhuang and, in the ninth

century, to the east along the Yellow River, in the region known as the Hexi corridor.

Congregations included women. Around 400 CE a female Manichaean missionary from Gaza, Julia, succumbed while struggling to preach the tenets of her faith to a hostile audience.[89] At the same time the elect were enjoined to regard female parishioners with caution. They were admonished to conform to a Parthian text that warned them to interact with women 'as a skilled craftsman deals with fire, using it for his purposes and not letting it burn him'.[90]

MANI THE PAINTER

Mani faced the challenge of gaining converts to his ideas in a world that was largely illiterate. Therefore, very early it became a part of Manichaean practice that much emphasis was placed on disseminating the faith through pictorial representations. Mani, himself a painter of some renown, is thought to have decorated the covers of the book describing his doctrines, called the *Arzhang*.[91] The followers of Mani were instructed to develop painting and sculpting skills to illustrate the canons of their faith with pictures and carvings. Disciples accompanied by multilingual scribes carried the illustrated words of Mani throughout the Middle East, the Roman Empire (extending to North Africa) and Central Asia.

PROSCRIPTION OF MANICHAEANISM

The ink-painted tapestries and carpets freighted to Japan had been strictly proscribed in China as trappings of Manichaeanism, the creed that had become anathema to China's Han rulers. Although there were numerous condemnations of the 'foreign' faith in the Song and Yuan dynasties,[92] China became increasingly xenophobic with the ascendance of the Ming Dynasty (1368–1644 CE). Hostility grew toward the Manichaean sect, which was

6.10

84

6.10

A series of multicoloured lifelike portraits of vegetables, including carrots, turnips, radishes and greens, appears beneath glowing diagonal crosses and jewel motifs. The vegetables decorate the roof and rafters of Chone Temple, Gansu Province.

perceived as non-Chinese and international in orientation.[93]

Chinese Confucians referred to the Manichaeans as 'vegetarian demon worshippers' and 'onion eaters'. It became common knowledge that they did not hold blood relationships sacred and paramount, but instead offered their primary loyalty to their fellow religionists. They entombed their corpses naked, contrary to the precepts of Confucianism.[94] Manichaeans were even criticised for their accomplishments in the carving and printing of wood blocks produced to disseminate their scriptures.

Even earlier, during the relatively tolerant rule of the Mongols, Manichaeans had increasingly become viewed as abnormal and offensive. During the Ming Dynasty this continuing affront to Chinese notions of propriety resulted in the widespread prohibition of Manichaean rites and trappings. Manichaean artworks were destroyed, although some works were salvaged to be sold and then shipped out of the country. For a long time this had been an acceptable practice for disposing of goods proscribed in China. The mindset that China was not only the 'middle country' but also the

6.11

6.11 (6.10)

The white robes of the Manichaean Elect covered them entirely. Men's hair was often dressed in long curls ('dreadlocks'). Women sometimes wore spit curls on their foreheads. Curly hair distinguished Uyghur Manichaeans them from the straight-haired Chinese and gave them pride. Reginald Ferrar, The Rainbow Bridge, London: E. Arnold, 1921, 75, after Klimkeit, 1982, Manichaean Art and Caligraphy, fig. 10a.

'only country' substantially aided the antique dealers and curio merchants seeking to acquire unique inventory for their overseas trade. Thousands of wardrobes holding exotic luxury dress and furnishings embellished with the symbols of deposed dynasties, including the Yuan, the Ming, and later the Qing, were sold, burned, or discarded.[95] Evidently this was fate of the Manichaean textiles. With each change in dynastic power, each decree of prohibition, willing traders freighted outlawed Manichaean trappings out of the Chinese universe to nearby foreign markets.

NOTES

74. Klimkeit, *Gnosis*, 3.

75. Jes Peter Asmussen, *Manichaean Literature: Representative Texts Chiefly from Middle Persian and Parthian Writings*, Persian Heritage Series 22 (Delmar, NY: Scholars' Facsimiles & Reprints, 1975), 6.

76. F. Crawford Burkitt, *The Religion of the Manichees*, Donnellan Lectures for 1924 (Cambridge: Cambridge University Press, 1925), 22; Klimkeit, *Gnosis*, 6.

77. Steven Runciman, *The Medieval Manichee: A Study of the Christian Dualist Heresy* (1947; repr., Cambridge: Cambridge University Press, 1982) 1, 13-14.

78. Asmussen, *Manichaean Literature*, 98, 103, 107.

79. Prof. Zhang Pengchuan told me that it was his understanding that the Uyghurs were settled in the Rongpo area from the eighth century on. Private communication, Suzhou, Jiangsu, China 2005.

80. Lieu, *Manichaeism in Central Asia*, 57–58.

81. An idea possibly borrowed from the Jains of India.

82. Lieu, Samuel N.C., *Manichaeism in the Later Roman Empire and Medieval China* (Manchester, UK: Manchester University Press, 1985), 277.

83. Takao Moriyasu, 'The Flourishing of Manichaeism under the West Uighur Kingdom. New Edition of the Uighur Charter on the Administration of the Manichaean Monastery in Qoco,' in *World History Reconsidered through the Silk Road*, Osaka University Twenty-First Century COE Program, Interface Humanities Research Activities 2002/2003 (Osaka, Japan: Osaka University, 2002), 80.

84. Klimkeit, *Gnosis*, 21.

85. Jason David BeDuhn, *The Manichaean Body: In Discipline and Ritual* (Baltimore: Johns Hopkins University Press, 2000), 189.

86. Klimkeit, *Gnosis*, 23.

87. Sharenkoff, *A Study of Manichaeism*, 6, 20.

88. Lieu, *Manichaeism in Central Asia*, 111.

89. Reported by Mark the Deacon to Bishop Porphyry of Gaza in Burkitt, *The Religion of the Manichees*, 8–10.

90. Klimkeit, *Manichaean Art*, 21.

91. Klimkeit, *Manichaean Art*, 14–16.

92. Lieu, *Manichaeism in Central Asia*, 129.

93. Lieu, *Manichaeism in Central Asia*, 153–55.

94. Oka Motoshi, 'Local Society in Southeastern Coastal Zhejiang and Manichaeism During the Song and Yuan Periods' (panel presentation, Interarea Session 27, Association for Asian Studies Conference, San Francisco, CA, April 6–9, 2006), 2.

95. Many of the surviving relics may now be viewed in the collections of North American, European, and Asian museums.

96. *Hometown of the Rainbow* 6, 74.

97. *Religion and Culture Around Xining China Tourism* August 1994 No.169, 36.

7

MANICHAEAN
MOTIFS

Both groups of 'mystery' textiles in the Kyoto Associations' collections – the ink-painted tapestries and the pile carpets – employ a range of decorative motifs that are associated with Manichaeanism, either through their resonance with the precepts of the religion, or through their documented appearance on known Manichaean architecture and artefacts.

THE CURLY GRASS MOTIF
The 'curly grass' motif is the most recognisable symbol of a Manichaean presence. The motif appears in a variety of forms on costume, carpets, temple interiors and exteriors, sculpture and furnishings. It is ubiquitous on Manichaean textiles. On the carpets woven for Living Buddhas the manes of the guardian dogs are composed of clusters of 'curly grass' motifs. Even the Mongol insignia of ram's horns, thought to bring increasing wealth, is created with two bold 'curly grass' motifs.

THE TREE OF LIFE
The Manichaean 'Tree of Life' appears as the main decorative element on six of the twenty-one audience carpets and as a

7.1
Ink-Painted Tapestry No.61.
A pair of affronted peacocks
surround the Manichaean
deities, the Sun and the Moon.
Western tradition sees a 'man
in the moon', but in East Asia it
is an image of a leaping rabbit
believed depicted on the moon.
Warp: 13 warps per 2.5 cm.
Weft: 28 wefts per 2.5 cm.
167 x 122 cm. Courtesy Iwatori
Boko Preservation Association.

7.2

7.3

7.4

7.5

7.6

88

7.2, 7.3, 7.4

The Tree of Life, documented and illustrated by Grünwedel, Klimkeit[107] and Moriyasu, and described by Lieu,[108] appears on tenth-century Manichaean cave paintings at Bezeklik in the Turfan region, now Xinjiang, China.[109]

minor motif on four of the ink-painted tapestries.[98] The three-trunked Tree of Life, covered with flowers and dripping with grape-like clusters, was a very recognisable symbol of Manichaean beliefs. It was referred to by opponents of Manichaeanism as 'that damned tree of the Manichaeans' (Birani).[99] In the Kyoto carpets, the apricot (not the plum) tree's three slender trunks have evolved into a tree with one abnormally thick and curving trunk rising from a curiously squared-off base [3.19, 3.29, 9.10]. The square base, which may represent a seat for Mani, is a unique feature in this group as the designers of these artworks generally avoided rectangles, right angles and straight lines.

GUARDIAN DOGS

Pairs of guardian dogs appear frequently on the tapestries and the carpets. Although commonly thought of as a Buddhist or Chinese motif, these canines have several distinctly Uyghur Manichaean features. The tail appears as a single, double or triple curl in the form of 'curly grass' motifs. The fur of the tails and manes

7.7

7.5
Detail, Ink–Painted Tapestry No.72. Apricot blossoms appear to float on the surface of Ink–Painted Tapestries Nos. 72 and 76, also suggesting the proximity of the Tree of Life. Courtesy Iwato Yama Preservation Association.

7.6
Triple Curly Grass Motif

7.7
Pile Carpet No.54. Tails and manes of the dogs are indicated with clusters of Curly Grass motifs and repeated thin lines. The dark animals run on a light gold ground, the use of which identifies the weavers or their clients as supporters of the then recently empowered Yellow Sect in this part of China. Warp: 7 warps per 2.5 cm. Weft: 12 wefts per 2.5 cm. 167 x 105 cm. Courtesy Naginata Boko Preservation Association.

7.8a

7.8b

7.8c

7.8d

7.8e

90

7.8a–e
Details, Ink-Painted Tapestry No.77. Leafy plant motifs and peony blossoms surround peacocks and cranes. The northwest tiger guards. Five cranes bestow longevity. The peacock protects from evil. The peony blossom suggests coming riches. Paired peacocks appear with guardian dogs and peonies. Courtesy Houka Boko Association.

is delineated with repeated black lines. The curls and repeated thin black lines are characteristic features of Uyghur Manichaean painting.[100]

THE PEACOCK

Birds considered auspicious to the Manichaeans appear repeatedly on the ink-painted tapestries. The most prominent and ubiquitous of these is the peacock. In Persia and elsewhere in the Middle East the peacock is known for its proclivity for finding and consuming snakes in orchards and gardens. Therefore it is

identified with the destruction of evil. Peacocks, carved and painted, were found at the entrances to temples and workshops [7.9]. Manichaean poetry and psalms include multiple references to the peacock:

The shining sun
and the glittering full moon
shine and glitter
from the trunk of this tree.
Brilliant birds
are there sporting happily.
Sporting (there) are doves (and)
peacocks of all colours.[101]

7.9

7.10

7.11

7.12

7.13

7.9

Carvings of peacocks appear on both sides of the entry pavilion at Chone Temple, once likely to have been a thriving Manichaean centre. Adjacent overhead beams are painted with images of leafy vegetation.

7.10

Detail, Ink-painted Tapestry No. 77. The magpie, considered a harbinger of a coming auspicious period, appears on several of the ink-painted tapestries. Multiple portraits of birds appear in Uyghur paintings and the aviary images continue to be important to their descendants, the Monguor. They embroider birds on their dress, paint them on their tapestries, and weave them into their carpets. Courtesy Houka Boko Association.

7.11

A ritual bouquet of peacock feathers stands beside artificial peonies in a permanent display at Upper Wutun Temple.

7.12

At Chone Temple shop in 2010, a feathered and electrified peacock model is offered for sale to visitors. When batteries are inserted in its base the bird's tail feathers spread wide as the bird emits a bloodcurdling shriek.

7.13

A Uyghur prince wears a robe with a repeat design of affronted peacocks. A wall painting with this type of portrait would normally be placed at the entries to cave temples. After Hartel and Yaldiz, Along the Ancient Silk Routes: Central Asian Art from the West Berlin State Museums (New York, Metropolitan Museum of Art 1982: 197, Fig 136. Courtesy Berlin Museum für Asiatischekunst.

91

7.14a

7.14b

7.14c

7.14d

7.14e

7.14f

7.14g

7.14

Details, Ink-Painted Tapestry No.61. Details include: a. Fret closure, b. Sun with curling clouds, c. Paired peacocks, d. Peony, e. Small bird on branch, f. Rabbit, standing for the moon, and g. Butterfly. Courtesy Niwa Tori Boko Preservation Association.

SQUASH MOTIFS

Certain fruits and vegetables were especially valued for their retention of light. These include melons, grapes, cucumbers, radishes and some types of squash. If uncut, kabocha squash retain their freshness and colour for many months after being removed from the vine, suggesting long healthy life. Squash were evidently a prized comestible.

The kabocha squash [7.16] was brought to Japan by the Portuguese in the 1500s, hence the vegetable's Japanese *katakana* name that translates as 'Cambodia' –

which is probably where the merchant mariners on their way to Japan first encountered them.[102] They were probably grown in the Yellow River region, since squash appear in Manichaean paintings and on the Kyoto carpets.

In one painting [7.17] of the Bema Festival, the most important Manichaean rite, can be seen a carpet depicted with a border showing cross sections of squash. A tripod bowl containing three layers of fruit and vegetables is arranged in a pyramid. Melons are visible at the bottom, then a layer of what appear to

7.15

7.16

7.17

7.15
*Detail, Pile Carpet No.39. The
border motif of cross sections of
squash on a Kyoto carpet. The
squash motif also appears on
the borders of Nos. 37 and 38.
Courtesy Minami Kannon Yama
Preservation Association.*

7.16
Kabocha squash.

7.17
*A tenth-century Manichaean
miniature painting uncovered in
Turfan depicts the Bema Festival,
the most important Manichaean
rite. The repeat motif on the
carpet border consists of cross
sections of squash (probably the
variety that came to be labelled
'kabocha' squash). Museum
für Asiatischekunst, Berlin.
MIKIII4979 a, b.*

7.19

7.18

7.20

7.21

7.18
The 'highlighted' Cross of Light found in Kizil near Kucha, documented by Klimkeit.[110]

be grapes, all topped by a type of green squash or gourd.[103]

Cross sections of squash are pictured on three of the earliest examples of pile carpets in Kyoto's Gion collections. The kabocha squash may have been deemed particularly attractive as the black-green outer shell encloses a bright orange pulp. Its rounded shape was probably found appealing, as curvilinear forms were a strong aesthetic preference of the Manichaean Uyghurs. The vegetable's colouration also suggests that it well suited the Manichaean practice of

utilising natural objects reflective of dark and light philosophy. Annemarie von Gabain describes this Manichaean aesthetic and illustrates it with drawings of a black-and-white appaloosa horse and with pomegranates whose white membranes enclose ruby-red seeds.[104]

THE CROSS OF LIGHT

The suffering Jesus, represented by the sum of light caught in matter and termed 'crucified light', was for the Manichaeans symbolised by a 'Cross of Light'. A Christian motif embraced by Manichaeans,

7.22

7.23

7.24

7.19

Partially obliterated diagonal crosses, Chone Temple, 2010. Sometime in the decade 1960–1970, The Red Brigades sought to obliterate the Manichaean crosses, using a form of turpentine. This was done at Chone Temple, and at both Wutun Temples. The Brigade members were apparently less offended by the 'riches-bestowing jewel' motifs painted on the finials of the support rafters.

7.20

Drawing of diagonal Manichaean crosses (Esin, 1967, Antecedents, 85, plate 1). On Upper Wutun Temple, Gansu Province, the glowing crosses are portrayed diagonally.

7.21

Detail of Pile Carpet No.47. The field of this carpet shows cooperating guardian dogs rolling a prayer cylinder that encloses the glowing Manichaean cross. The motif also appears on the costumes of sprites portrayed on Manichaean paintings found in Turfan (Gulácsi 2005). Courtesy Naginata Boko Preservation Association.

7.22

A large diagonal Manichaean cross appears at the end of each support beam at Chone Temple. The peacock's presence is indicated by the bird's feathers painted above; and below are peonies, jewels and Curly Grass motifs.

7.23

Detail of cornerstone with incised and highlighted Manichaean cross, Guanghua Temple, Guanting County, Qinghai Province.

7.24

A glowing Manichaean cross appears below Curly Grass and spiral motifs at Rongpo Gonchen Temple, Tongren.

95

7.25

7.26

7.25

Detail of Ink-Painted Tapestry No. 68. A translucent jellyfish swims among marine plants, lotus, and peony buds. See Fig. 9.1. Courtesy Tsuki Boko Preservation Association.

7.26

Guanghua Temple, Guanting County, a Monguor temple in Qinghai Province.

the Cross of Light is often illustrated with highlighted and slightly off-kilter glowing bars, resembling neon lighting.

The Manichaean cross may be seen in the Monguor country in Gansu province; painted on temple murals at Rongpo Temple, Tongren; on finials at Chone Temple and Upper Wutun Temple; and incised into the foundation stone at Guanghua Temple, Guanting.[105] The cross on these structures is invariably a glowing cross.

During the Cultural Revolution zealots of the Red Brigades apparently rubbed a turpentine-like solution over the crosses in an attempt to obliterate them. This must have been a challenging task as the crosses appear above the second storey of the temple.[106]

NOTES

98. Lieu, *Manichaeism in Central Asia,* 20–21.

99. It is thought that the Buddhist concept of the jewelled tree is closely connected to this tree; Klimkeit, *Manichaean Art,* 31.

100. Russell-Smith, *Uygur Patronage,* 111, 114, 120, 142.

101. Heinrich F.J. Junker, 'Mittelpers. fraš̄emurv 'Pfau',' *Wörter und Sachen* 12 (1929): 132, quoted in Asmussen, *Manichaean Literature,* 38.

102. Apparently squash have been categorised as a New World vegetable but, if that is the case, how is it that squash and gourds appear in tenth-century Manichaean paintings and on the pile carpets woven in the fourteenth to fifteenth centuries in Gansu-Qinghai provinces, China?

103. BeDuhn, *The Manichaean Body,* 156.

104. Annemarie Gabain, *Uigurischen Konigreich,* fig. 14, fig. 56.

105. Moriyasu, 'Flourishing of Manichaeism,' fig. 4.

106. Locals informed me that, although the Red Brigades had trucks that enabled them to get to the remote mountain locations of the Manichaean temples, they did not bring extension ladders.

107. Klimkeit, *Manichaean Art,* 31, plate 11.

108. Lieu, *Later Roman Empire.*

109. Moriyasu, 'Flourishing of Manichaeism,' 5–7; panel 16 photographed by the author; panel 17 sketched by A. Jacovleff in 1931 (originally published in Joseph Hackin, *Recherches archéologiques en Asie Centrale,* Paris: Éditions d'art et d'histoire, 1931, pl. 1); panel 18 sketched by Albert Grünwedel (originally published in Grünwedel, *Alt-Kutscha,* Berlin: O. Elsner, 1920, fig. 66).

110. Klimkeit, *Manichaean Art,* plate 11, fig. 16.

8

TIME, SPACE AND TERMINOLOGY

By 2010 I felt I had made several significant steps towards discovering the origins of the textiles. But, as I scanned the map of East Asia, there were three major obstacles barring my quest to determine their true provenance:

1. Time: five centuries had passed;

2. Space: the vastness of China and the complexity of its population;

3. Change: every town, river, mountain, borderline and people in China appeared to have altered its name with changes in the government. Entire communities had changed their religion.

A number of questions had not been answered: precisely where had the ink-painted tapestries been designed, woven and painted? Were the weavers also the painters? Where had the pile carpets been knotted? Who were the weavers who created the carpets, and what happened to them? What was the meaning, if any, of their extraordinary designs? Why did my investigations provoke animosity? Why did they make Chinese as well as Japanese scholars so uncomfortable?

The answers uncovered were sparse and negative. The artworks were not Korean

Detail of Fig. 11.5. Ink-painted tapestry. The Manichaean peacock is in the process of being replaced by the Taoists' crane.

8.2

(although a Japanese functionary had travelled on to Korea on several occasions in an effort to persuade the Koreans they were the makers). In China, the suggestion of a Uyghur attribution provoked a stony silence. The Chinese I met did not seem to want to know much about them. In that land a reaction of mild disgust met most of my enquiries. A professor from Xinjiang actually became enraged at my queries, pursed her lips, turned her back on me, and refused to continue the conversation, after declaring that the contentious Uyghur people could not possibly produce artwork worthy of admiration.[111]

Ignoring these discouraging responses, and despite the centuries that had passed since the artworks were created, I had faith that some fragmentary evidence or related relics would be located in or near the site of their production. Just as humans must leave footprints, cultures must leave artefacts. In the fine arts, styles sway with artists' talent and innovations, or respond to clients' influence, as well as to political or economic events. In the cultural arts, styles, and particularly motifs, are handed down from parent to child or passed along by the craftspeople of a community.

Moreover it seemed that in China, up until the late twentieth century, many families have remained in or near their ancestral home towns through centuries of turmoil and upheaval.[112] This is in contrast to the situation in my American homeland. Family registers are frequently salvaged. It is not unusual for an ordinary Chinese citizen to believe that he or she has a firm grasp of the threads of his ancestral history.

BEYOND CHINA: INK-PAINTED TAPESTRIES IN MUSEUM COLLECTIONS

Although most American citizens do not keep family registers, official western institutions do attempt to preserve records.

I searched the records I could locate outside of China. In addition to the renowned collections in Kyoto, collections of ink-painted tapestries are held by a few other institutions in Japan, including one in the town of Ötsu, near Kyoto. At the Honolulu Academy of the Arts, 'Old China Hands' (foreigners long established in the country) and their descendants had bestowed typical late Ming and Qing dynasty examples of the ink-painted tapestries on that collection.[113] Somewhat unexpectedly, other European and American institutions also quite often possess one or two examples of the ink-painted tapestries. These were produced in the later splinter sites established on the south China coast.

Interestingly, in each institution worldwide, a different provenance and function is cited. It was only in the 1989 records of the Museum of Oriental Art in Moscow that a notation appeared that seemed to accord with the discoveries my research had produced. In Moscow a Russian ethnologist had labelled the ink-painted tapestries 'Uyghur', giving support to my most promising theory. The Russians were not only proximate to the area of the textiles' probable production in China but, also, Russian explorers were among the first to investigate northwest Chinese societies in the late nineteenth century.

Back in northern Japan, the Tohoku Fukushi University's Serizawa Keisuke Art and Craft Museum in Sendai had documented later examples of the ink-painted tapestries that had found their way into their collection via Ainu tribespeople. The Ainu, indigenous people of Japan, participated in a canoe trade route between northeast China, Sakhalin Island and northern Japan.[114] The late Japanese scholar Serizawa Chosuke, then director of the Museum, among others, encouraged me to look again to China as the source of the earlier ink-painted tapestries. Some

8.2

Ainu matron wearing a Chinese imperial silk tapestry (kesi) robe seated on an Ink-painted Tapestry, c. 1700–1750 CE. The tapestry appears to have the design of five cranes. Painted by Kojima Sessai after an original by Kaizaki Hakyo (1764–1826 CE), painter of an Ainu portrait series around 1790 CE. .

8.3

Chinese silk brocades and some tapestry-woven silk textiles (*kesi*) preserved in Japan are said to have been carried there by Ainu seafarers. These textiles are called *ezo nishiki*, a strange appellation that translates as 'Ainu silk brocade'. The Ainu tribes did not have any access to raw silk and did not weave with silk. They did, however, obtain Chinese silk textiles from ocean traders in the form of garments and also from fragments culled from discarded furnishings. The Ainu sometimes appliquéd these scraps on their elm-bark robes.

Prof. Ohtsuka Kazuyoshi and his colleagues at the Osaka Museum of Ethnology had traced the Chinese textiles carried from the Ming and Qing dynasties to a 'northern Silk Route'. The path was used to forward the Chinese textiles, outlawed when dynastic governments changed hands, across northern China via a river and sea route – the Heilongjiang River (China), the Amur River (Japan) and Sakhalin Island – to merchants in northern Japan.[115] Several examples are preserved and exhibited in Hokkaido and northern Honshu.

8.3
*Ainu man wearing trade goods consisting of a Chinese imperial silk robe (*kesi*) under a Russian cloth overcoat. Kojima Sessai after an original by Kaizaki Hakyo (1764–1826 CE), painter of the portrait series around 1790 CE. The Matsuura Historical Museum, Hokkaido, has a copy of the series as does the Museé d'Ethnographie et Histoire Naturelle, in Besançon, France.*

NOTES

111. For that academic, the Uyghurs represented uncivilised and extremist behaviour that no artistic accomplishment could offset.

112. Schram, *The Monguors*, vol. 3, 16.

113. 'Old China Hands' generally refers to Americans and Europeans engaged in the 18th to 20th century trade with Chinese merchants in China's port cities and in Hawaii

114. Chosuke Serizawa, *Ainu Bunkaten* [Exhibition of Ainu Culture], (Sendai: Tohoku Fukushi Daigaku Serizawa Keisuke Bijutsu Kōgeikan, 1990), 163–94.

115. Kazuyoshi Ohtsuka, *Ainu Moshiri: Minzoku Mon'you kara Mita Ainu no Sekai* [The world of the Ainu through their design motifs] (Osaka: National Museum of Ethnology, 1993), 60–61.

9
THE MONGUOR

TURKO-MONGOL BUDDHISTS OF NORTHWEST CHINA

Costume often retains motifs discarded in other art forms. Convinced that historic costume might yield important clues, in 2000 I began to study the dress of China's almost sixty minority groups. In a comprehensive volume illustrating their characteristics, I found costumes with designs that echoed those on the ink-painted tapestries and carpets in Kyoto.[116] They belonged to the Monguor, a northwest Chinese minority.

THE MONGUOR MINORITY
Prof. Keith W. Slater has described the perplexities surrounding the precise origins of the Monguor.[117] In his informative book *A Grammar of Mangghuer: A Mongolic Language of China's Qinghai-Gansu Sprachbund,* he discusses the various theories proposed by scholars.

Prof. Slater describes a country that is a mixture of Mongols, Turkic Uyghurs, Tibetans and Chinese, who inhabit the region and whose languages and cultures come into contact there. He explains that, from the Chinese perspective, the Monguor region serves as both the frontier with Inner Asia and the border with Tibet. The Chinese settlers founded their communities

9.1
Ink-Painted Tapestry No.68. A translucent jellyfish swims around the peony and lotus buds, past leafy clusters. Curly Grass motifs extend from the plant stems.
Warp: 10 warps per 2.5 cm.
Weft: 25 wefts per 2.5 cm.
162 x 112 cm. Courtesy Tsuki Boko Preservation Association

9.2

9.3

106

9.2

Map: The Land of the Monguor.

9.3

A Monguor woman proudly displays her Tibetan-inspired outer garment with its long sleeves of the five colours. Although today the Monguor fervently profess Tibetan Buddhism, motifs on their costumes reflect earlier Manichaean ideas as well. Huzhu, Qinghai 1998.

in the lower elevations. In the north and northeast there are Mongol tribes. In the desert-like environment that stretches to the northwest there are Turkic Uyghur communities. Another Turkic people, the Shatto, joined these communities, possibly because they felt comfortable living among a people with a Turkic culture.

The Monguor, however, appear to prefer to identify with their Mongol forebears and they speak a Mongol dialect. Few Turkic words are retained in their language.[118] Nevertheless costume, textiles and architecture reflect their Uyghur Turkic legacy. Many also speak Chinese, especially the younger people who have attended school.

Much of the Monguor population lives in eastern Qinghai and Gansu provinces, in settlements along the Yellow River, the main transport system in the area until recent times. The area represents a transition in elevation, as the steppes of north central China give way to high mountain ranges, divided by river valleys. The river forms the boundary between Qinghai and Gansu. Connecting the Monguor settlements, it served as the

9.4

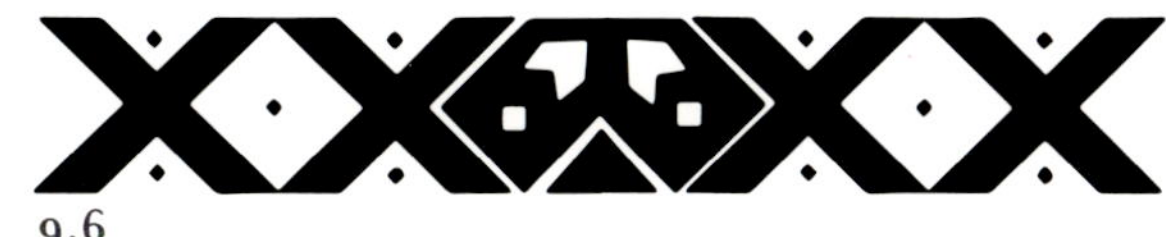

9.6

9.5

9.7

9.8

9.9

9.4
The Uyghur Manichaean Curly Grass motif is embroidered and appliquéd on shoes for a Monguor man, twentieth century. After Shanghai Theatrical College, Ethnic Costumes, 64, fig. 138.

9.5
A young Monguor mother wearing a traditional hat in a style inherited from her Mongol ancestors. This hat, worn conspicuously outside the home, may be seen at all times in the Monguor country. Her cotton indigo-dyed upper garment and trousers are those worn by Chinese in villages in the countryside.

9.6
Inner border design of Pile Carpet No. 47, c. thirteenth century. The unusual design seen on the inner border of this carpet also appears embroidered on traditional Monguor hats.[130]

9.7
The top of a Monguor hat embroidered at the centre with a geometric design that resembles that seen on the Monguor audience carpets preserved in Kyoto. After Editorial Committee of Shanghai Theatrical College, Ethnic Costumes and Clothing Decorations from China, Hong Kong: Hai Feng, 1986, 66.

9.8, 9.9
The cult of the White Tiger continues to be important in the Monguor region. Portraits of the animal may be seen guarding the entryway of most homes.[131]

108 9.10
Pile Carpet No.43. The Tree of Life, along with the popular local northwest Chinese talisman the White Tiger, appears on this audience carpet. In the corners appear the ram horns, a Turko–Mongol motif bestowing wishes for increasing wealth (i.e., increasing herds).[132] *Warp: 6 warps per 2.5 cm. Weft: 4 wefts per 2.5 cm. 185 x 110 cm. Courtesy Kanko Boko Preservation Association.*

9.11

9.12

Monguors' main transport system during the Yuan and Ming dynasties. Goods were carried by raft, boat and pack animal from Yellow River communities toward the seaports on the Pacific.[119]

Today the Monguor live on both banks of the Yellow River and on both banks of its tributary, the Datong River. They also live in six or seven towns in the region, including Xining, capital of Qinghai province, in Huzhu, Minhe and also in Datong county of Qinghai province. A few more are scattered in Ledu and Menyuan counties and in the Tianzhu Tibetan autonomous province, as well as in Yongdeng and Linxia in Gansu province.

There is general agreement that the Monguor have been living in the region since at least the Yuan dynasty (1271–1368 CE). Historical records based on the annals of the city of Xining and the province of Qinghai were translated and reported by the most dedicated of scholars, Louis M.J. Schram, a CICM missionary who lived and studied among the Monguor for eleven years from 1911–22 CE, and published three detailed and illustrated volumes on their history and culture.[120] He recites the story

9.11
A carved and painted baffle found in the Monguor country reveals a continuing dedication to curvilinear forms and vibrant colour.

9.12
An offering table swathed in imported silk brocades is adorned with fresh and preserved fruits cherished by the Monguor, and an exotic imported drink. A lengthy printed silk presentation scarf (kata), drapes the throne for a High Lama at Wutun Monastery.

9.13

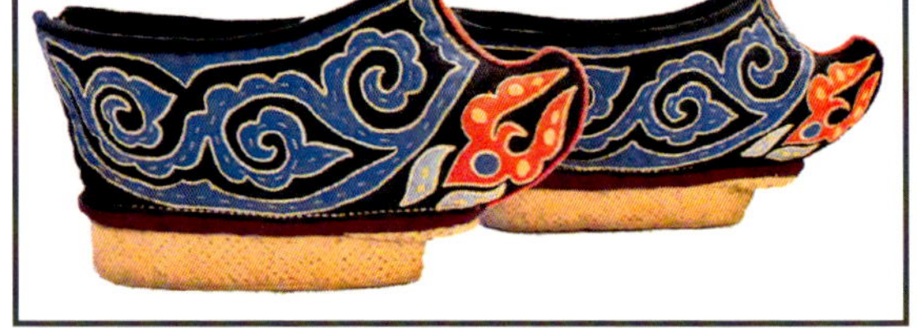

9.15

9.14

9.16

9.13
A Monguor man wears a vest embroidered with full-blown peonies.

9.14
Framed and embroidered silk and cotton panel from a Monguor woman's costume, twentieth century. The safeguarding peacock stands on a branch filled with fortuitous peony blossoms.

of the sixteen Monguor clans, describing each clan's submission to the Ming Chinese when they took over from the Yuan Mongols. Father Schram concludes his lengthy efforts to determine Monguor origins with a quote from Li Ming, High Lama and Superintendent of Youning Temple, the most important educational institution in the area. High Lama Li Ming responded to his queries regarding the origin of the Monguor by declaring, 'the Monguor are all of Uyghur origin!'[121]

The Monguor citizens I met and spoke with in the last decade of the

twentieth century and the first decade of the twenty-first century generally believe that their families have inhabited the area since their ancestors first settled in Ganzhou more than 800 years ago. Subutai, one of Genghis Khan's most prized generals, arrived in the region and there encountered a population the Tibetans refer to as 'Hor', their term for 'Uyghur'. This encounter and the marriages that were eventually consummated between Mongol warriors and Uyghur women led to the formation of the Monguor people.

9.17

9.18

9.19

9.20

9.15
Reverse appliqué technique may be seen on these shoes worn by an adult Monguor woman; they are c. 1950, 17.5 cm long. The Chinese practice of footbinding was imitated by women in some Monguor clans. Reverse appliqué technique embellishes Monguor wardrobes and is even replicated on the decorative murals that adorn a Xining mosque, painted by Monguors in the first half of the twentieth century. Courtesy private collection.

9.16
Monguor embroidered bag, twentieth century. A pair of stylised peacocks appears above cooperating guardian dogs sheltered by peony buds and blossoms. Motifs are typically highlighted on Monguor embroidery.

9.17
Embroidered plaque, Monguor woman's costume, twentieth century. The corner details replicate those appearing as corner details on the carpets preserved in Kyoto. After Shanghai Theatrical College, Ethnic Costumes, *66, fig. 144.*

9.18
Panel from a woman's costume, embroidered with a running Curly Grass motif, twentieth century. (Shanghai Theatrical College, Ethnic Costumes, *66, figure 144.)*

9.19
Ink-Painted Tapestry No.84. Curving branches of the Tree of Life appear on both end panels, each sheltering a string of four doves. The doves' bodies alternate between Dark and Light as do the paired guardian dogs in the centre circle. Ovoid forms may suggest Light swallowing Dark. The tails of all the guardian dogs in this example are composed of three Curly Grass motifs. On both end panels the White Tiger is seen glaring agressively out at the viewer. Warp: 9 warps per 2.5 cm. Weft: 32 wefts per 2.5 cm. 158 x 80 cm. Courtesy Houka Boko Preservation Association.

9.20
Detail, Ink-Painted Tapestry No.83. The feather images indicate the presence of auspicious birds. Courtesy Houka Boko Preservation Association.

9.21

9.21
*Rongpo Gonchen Temple,
Tongren, Gansu Province.*

9.22
*Ink-Painted Tapestry No.74.
Magpies are thought to be
chattering about auspicious
tidings. Five cranes by broad-
leaved plants may represent the
five sons of Mani. As a Taoist
image, the crane, reputed to
live 1,000 years, represents
longevity and is said to be the
conveyance of the Taoist hermit-
sages as they flew through the
heavens. Crane portraits appear
throughout the ink-painted
tapestries from the earliest to the
latest examples. Courtesy Houka
Boko Preservation Association.*

Although the Mongols were victorious
warriors and powerful rulers, they admired
the literacy and artistic abilities, as well as
the military prowess, of the Uyghur people.
They allowed the Monguor clan leaders,
the *Tusi*, to continue in their local governing
roles and, further, gave them official
status as resident administrators under the
aegis of the Mongols. During the Yuan
dynasty, the Monguor and their ancestors,
the Uyghur, were categorised as *semu*, a
class just beneath the Mongols and above
the Chinese. The Uyghur *semu* were
often given appointments not only as

administrators but also as auxiliary
government workers.

There is much confusion and little
documentation as to what degree of
assimilation actually went on in the
Mongol-Uyghur communities. However,
it is irrefutable that Uyghur stylistic traits
and Uyghur Manichaean motifs are
ubiquitous on Monguor dress and temple
architecture to the present time.

The present-day overt and predominant
religion of the Monguor people is Tibetan
(Lamaist) Buddhism. Before 1723 CE the
Lamaist monasteries were very wealthy and

9.22

9.23

powerful. The Mongols supported the institutions and expected the lamas' help in controlling the population. The monasteries derived considerable income from tax and rent. They owned herds of sheep, cattle and horses. Oil and grain mills provided additional revenue. The most lucrative economic activity of the monasteries was the business of finance itself. The monks were moneylenders to the entire population of the region.[122] A region-wide revolution in 1723 CE significantly diminished the power of the monks and monasteries. Since the establishment of the People's Republic in 1949, many formerly active monasteries have become nearly vacant and most are viewed by mainstream Chinese people as curious relics of the past.

Although most of the Monguor people profess Tibetan Buddhism, it seems that Manichaean concepts have nevertheless survived underground in a small percentage of the population. Designs on costumes and furnishings continue to depict Manichaean values such as the duality of light and dark. The 'curly grass' motif (a treasured Uyghur image) remains popular,

9.23

Detail, Ink-Painted Tapestry No.82. Did the same artisans skilfully weave the tapestries and elaborately paint them? It seemed plausible that Qinzhou, the renowned tapestry-weaving centre with its spacious workshops, was capable of producing the ink-painted tapestries, probably including those shipped to Japan in earlier centuries. Courtesy Naginata Boko Preservation Association.

113

9.24

9.24

Upper Wutun Monastery, Gansu Province, is surrounded by manicured gardens as well as abundant and impressive statuary. The interior walls are filled with murals and tangka picturing the meditational dieties.

and the ever-present Manichaean talisman the peacock is still being embroidered on garments worn by both sexes.

The Monguor people were originally herders, raising sheep and goats and practising the nomadic lifestyle they had known in their former communities in Ganzhou and Mongolia. In Gansu and Qinghai they were strongly encouraged by the Chinese Government to give up animal husbandry and take up farming. At present they subsist by growing wheat and barley. Wool is collected from sheep and yaks and taken to Chinese government-supervised factories, where knitwear and weavings of multiple kinds are produced and sold.[123] Their wool carpets are designed for the commercial market, most of them tapping western designs and colours deemed fashionable in China. A few carpets incorporate traditional Monguor or Mongol motifs such as the peony.

MONGUOR ARTISTS PAINT A MOSQUE

My explorations were not producing sufficient evidence that the weavers and painters in China were responsible for the carpet and tapestry examples preserved in

9.25

9.26

9.27

9.25
Most architectural features at the Wutun monasteries are covered with bright paint. This temple doorway seems to have suffered attempts to scrape it clean of the original surface decoration. The underlying wood carving, resembling but not the same as the Manichaean Curly Grass motifs, are still visible. Similar vegetal motifs are seen on a drawing of the tall hat worn by a Manichaean Elect are described by Gulácsi as 'plant scroll motifs'. [6.2].

9.26
In the Wutun community of Niandehu (Ch), the cult of the white tiger remains strong. At nearby Upper Wutun Monastery the monks sleep on platforms sitting on bedframes embellished with tiger stripes. The tiger is believed powerful enough to disperse harmful spirits.

9.27
Mural illustrating the Wutu, seemingly as female figures, depicted with large breasts and long hair, at the recently constructed Regong Hotel, Tongren County, China.

9.29

9.28

9.30

116

9.28

Archway leading to Upper Wutun Temple.

Kyoto. I had found descendants of the Uyghur and Mongol peoples in the Monguor people of Gansu and Qinghai provinces. Features of their dress and architecture indicated strong design connections to the ink-painted tapestries as well as to the carpets.

A reflection of the Monguors' long-standing wide reputation as especially skilled painters arrived from a surprising source. In Xining City I learned that it was not Muslim but Monguor artists and artisans who were chosen to adorn the Great Mosque of the eastern suburb of

Xining when it was extensively renovated in 1926–46 CE.[124] The motifs painted across the walls of the Mosque annex are identical in style to the reverse appliqué work that embellishes much of traditional Monguor dress. The reputation of Monguor artists survived through to the twentieth century.

Everywhere in the Monguor country it was stated repeatedly that that the Monguor once wove in abundance on home looms, but since the 1950s nearly all wool weaving has taken place and is supervised in China's government factories. Current scholars

9.32

9.31

9.33

9.29
The Assembly Hall of Upper Wutun Monastery presents typical Tibetan Buddhist temple architecture. The bright yellow paint covering the buildings reflects the temple's continuing loyalty to the Buddhist Yellow Hat Sect.

9.30
The many gardens that dot Upper Wutun Monastery are filled with blossoms of especially vibrant hues, including marigolds, poppies, asters and zinnias.

9.31
A painting academy, The College of Regong Arts (identified in an English Language doorway sign beneath its Chinese characters), has been established at Upper Wutun Monastery. It accepts apprentices from several lands who will master the skills required to paint mandala, thangka and Buddhist murals.

9.32
Upper Wutun Monastery's Assembly Hall exemplifies the typical style, design and colour spectrum seen in the region.

9.33
A lone monk strolls just before dusk at Upper Wutun Monastery.

9.35

9.36

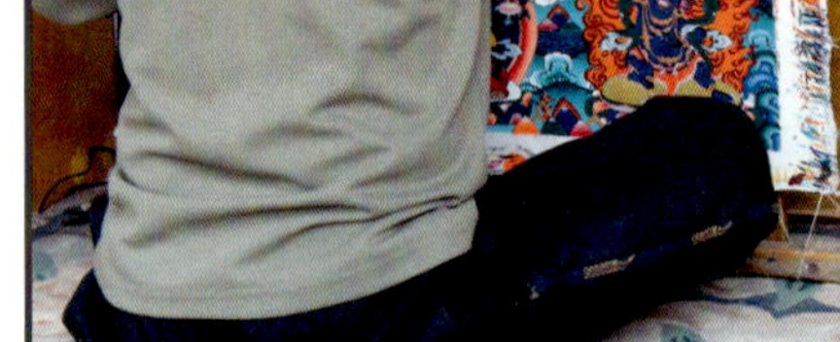

9.37

9.34

Wutun paintings often emphasise the attributes of the bodhisattva Avalokitesvara of the Thousand Eyes and Thousand Arms. The bodhisattva, thought to be Protector of Sight, has been continuously popular in both the Uyghur and Monguor communities.

who had done research among the Monguor were sceptical that the Monguor, relatively impoverished village farmers in recent centuries, were responsible for the large and complex ink-painted tapestries filled with philosophical imagery. The ink-painted tapestries appear to be the product of a long line of highly skilled artisans, working at large looms in a spacious urban environment.

Who were the fine painters who dedicated themselves to embellishing the surfaces of the wool tapestries with ink pen and coloured dyes over a 400-year period?

It is possible the weavers were also the painters, though this is not known. It was certainly true that the ink-painted and woven areas were planned more or less simultaneously, before production, as the painted details serve to elaborate and complete the forms established by the woven segments.

At that point in my research trip I came across a helpful guidebook.[125] It described long-standing colonies of professional painters living for hundreds of years in five Monguor villages called Wutun in the environs of Rongpo Gonchen Monastery in

9.38

9.39

9.40

9.35
Roofed open-air corridor sheltering prayer cylinders at Upper Wutun Monastery.

9.36
Glowing Manichaean diagonal crosses once embellished the rafters at Upper Wutun Monastery. During the Cultural Revolution (1966–76 CE), members of the Red Brigades made a partially successful attempt to remove them using a turpentine-like substance.

9.37
Thangka painter at Upper Wutun Monastery.

9.38
Seemingly endless pastoral scenes surround Chone Monastery, Qinghai Province. Shepherds tend sheep, yaks and cattle.

9.39
Chone Temple's subdued entry pavilion belies a continuing array of brilliant hues along the roof, the eaves, the rafters, and throughout the interiors.

9.40
Peony P. rockii cultivated at Chone Monastery. Monguor monks may have cultivated this peony to illustrate the Light and Dark precepts of the Manichaean religion.

9.41

9.42

9.41

Features of the peacock and components of its feathers, along with jewels, diagonal crosses and peony motifs, extend to the highest roof peaks at Chone Temple.

the city of Tongren, Gansu province. The important monastery had been established there during the Yuan dynasty in 1301 CE, an interlude when Manichaeans were able to practise their faith. That freedom would be largely curtailed with the arrival of the second Ming government at the end of the fourteenth century.

THE PAINTERS OF WUTUN

Upper Wutun Monastery was established in 1385, a few decades after Rongpo Gonchen Monastery in Tongren. It is famed for its Tibeto-Chinese architecture and its extensive sculpture and painted murals. The author of the guidebook on the region describes the nearby Wutun villages as having each and every male inhabitant professionally occupied with skilled sculpture or fine painting. The artists create statues and murals of the meditational deities for temples as well as *tangka* (portable paintings) catering to enthusiastic private clients throughout the region.[126] Their fame is widespread. For centuries custom orders have continuously arrived in the Wutun villages from as far away as Nepal and India.[127]

9.43

9.44

9.42
*Chone Monastery, Gansu
Province. Faithful renditions of
vegetables — including turnips,
raddishes, carrots, and leafy
greens — appear protected
between the roof support beams
of the entry pavilion to Chone
Temple. The Manichaeans were
strict vegetarians.*

9.43
*The rafter finials represent
varicoloured shining gems.
Below may be seen full-blown
peonies painted cerulean blue,
gold, white and raspberry.
A series of crosses, smudged
with turpentine, survive
above the painted gems. The
highlighted Curly Grass motifs
on the cross-beams assume a
rectangular format, their right
angles a highly unusual choice
for Manichaean artists, and
probably reflective of growing
Chinese stylistic influence.*

9.44
*Support beams are adorned
with auspicious motifs, including
the ubiquitous highlighted
Curly Grass motif, seen above
a row of highlighted diagonal
crosses. Panels are painted with
Tibetan prayers. Chone Temple,
Gansu Province.*

9·45

122

9·45

The voluminously feathered Manichaean guardian charged with the forestalling of evil, the peacock, is carved and painted in sculptures affronté on either side of the entry way to Chone Temple.

In 2007 I left the provincial capital city of Lanzhou and hastened to the Wutun 'painters' villages' to meet with local artists. These included the affable Tse Rong Jya, his wife and his painter son, Wan Ne TseRong, in the village of Nianduhu. They said their ancestral family had lived in the region for over 500 years. Tse Rong Jya described six or seven generations of his male forebears who had been fine painters. They had all been born in the area but it was his belief that members of his family had emigrated earlier from Ganzhou (present day Zhangye), the capital of the Uyghur Empire.

The Ganzhou Uyghur Kingdom existed from 870 to 1036 CE.

In the Wutun community of Nianduhu, the cult of the white tiger remains strong. At nearby Upper Wutun Monastery the monks sleep on carpeted platforms whose frames are also embellished with tiger stripes. It is believed that the tiger has the strength to repel illness. The tiger's protective role is honoured each November at the Wutu Festival.[128] Male dancers parade and promenade in tiger make-up while performing ritual ablutions.[129] During my visit in 2010 I was surprised to see fresh murals celebrating the Wutu performance on the spanking new walls of the glamorous four-star Regong Tourist Hotel. On these murals, for reasons not explained, the virile male dancers are represented as females with protruding breasts and long hair.

Chhaya Bhattachaya-Haesner has documented the role of the Thousand-Armed and Thousand-Eyed Avalokitesvara as a cult figure to the Uyghurs, a role in which the bodhisattva seemingly persists for their descendants, the Monguor. Imagery linked to the bodhisattva and her attributes are ubiquitous subjects on the Wutun *tangkas* and temple murals.

Avalokitesvara is particularly referenced by eyes, single, multiple, serial and separated [9.34]. The bodhisattva is believed to have the power to cure eye diseases. Reiterating the shape of the eyes, sparkling gems line up, resembling dyed Easter eggs. Many references to the jewels also appear on the textiles in Kyoto, including a 'net of jewels' motif associated with Tibetan Buddhist imagery. Silk Road merchants sometimes carried their actual jewels sewn in netting, possibly engendering the motif.

NOTES

116. Editorial Committee of Shanghai Theatrical College, *Ethnic Costumes and Clothing Decorations from China.* (Hong Kong: Hai Feng, 1986), 62–64, Plates 138, 142c,144,151–53. See also Central Academy of Ethnology, ed., *Costumes of the Minority Peoples of China* (Kyoto: Binobi, 1982).

117. Some authorities, including Prof. Slater, have labelled the Monguor *Mangghuer*, a term used in Minhe county, Qinghai province, and what the people call themselves in that location.

118. Personal communication with Keith W. Slater, Lanzhou, China, September 30, 2006.

119. Schram, *The Monguors*, vol. 1, 19

120. Schram, *The Mongours.*

121. Schram, *The Mongours*, vol. 1, 27.

122. Henry Schwarz, *The Minorities of Northern China A Survey* (Bellingham, WA: Western Washington University, 1984), 115.

123. Actually it appears that there exists some negativity toward yak herding or yak products. When I first began visiting the area in the last decade of the twentieth century, multiple high quality yak wool goods were offered for sale. The yak sweaters, scarves and tights, incredibly warm and comfortable, have mysteriously disappeared from the stores in recent years.

124. Piper Rae Gaubatz, *Beyond the Great Wall: Urban Form and Transformation on the Chinese Frontiers* (Stanford, CA: Stanford University Press, 1996), 222.

125. Gyurme Dorje, *Footprint Tibet.* 608–09.

126. Andreas Gruschke, *The Cultural Monuments of Tibet's Outer Provinces: Amdo*, vol. 1, *The Qinghai Part of Amdo* (Bangkok: White Lotus, 2001), 55–58.

127. It is reported that, during the years of persecution, Manichaean painters also found refuge in the Ladakh, India region of the then Tibetan Empire; (see Klimkeit, *Manichaean Art*, 20.) A cape with Curly Grass motifs in the reverse appliqué technique favoured by the Monguors is worn not far from the elaborately painted caves at Alchi. Monisha Ahmed, *Living Fabric: Weaving among the Nomads of Ladakh Himalaya* (Bangkok: Orchid, 2002), 115, fig 119.

128. I had seen the rivetting 'Wutu' with their tiger stripe-painted bodies in a video of the festival produced by the ethnographer and linguistics specialist Prof. Kevin Stuart and his colleagues.

129. Zhu Yongzhong recorded this 'ritual winter exorcism' on 8mm camcorder in Gnyan thog village, Qinghai Province, on December 30 1996. A copy of this video ('Wutu,' running time 31:05) was uploaded to YouTube on May 3 2011, and can be accessed at https://www.youtube.com/watch?v=1PMthBldYYo. See also Kalsang Norbu, Zhu Yongzhong, and Kevin Stuart, 'A Ritual Winter Exorcism in Gnyan Thog Village, Qinghai', *Asian Folklore Studies* 58 (1999): 189–203.

130. Wang, *Chinese Costume.*

131. Schram, *The Monguors*, vol. 2, 87–88.

132. Schram, *The Monguors*, vol. 2, 87–88.

10 CHARACTERISTICS OF THE KYOTO TAPESTRIES

Some of the thirty-six ink-painted wool tapestries appear to have been woven in pairs, though no two are exactly alike.[133] There are many single examples as well. It is unknown whether at times only one was produced or if its 'mate' was lost or destroyed.

ARTISANS

The ink-painted tapestries were woven by men. In towns with Monguor populations a male professional weaver visited the communities, set up his loom, and produced what the villagers required.

TECHNIQUE

Weft-faced tapestry technique with single dovetailing [10.6] was employed to create these weavings. In tapestry with single dovetailing, adjacent colours of weft yarns turn on a single warp. There are few slits left open between adjacent colours, but most are closed.[134] The curvilinear pictorial subjects were created by means of the insertion of eccentric wefts. This non-rectilinear tapestry technique is termed 'eccentric weave'. The main subjects of the tapestries and their colour blocks were planned and arranged before any weaving got underway.

Ink-Painted Tapestry No.62. The head, neck and part of the body of the peacock and its feathers in this tapestry, as well as the surrounding cranes, were created by means of the insertion of eccentric wefts. Courtesy Tsuki Boko Preservation Association.

10.2

10.3

10.2

Detail of Ink-Painted Tapestry No.79. On the ink-painted tapestries the guardian dogs are over time portrayed as increasingly menacing. Their gaping jaws reveal barred fangs. Courtesy Kanko Boko Preservation Association.

10.3

Detail of Ink-Painted Tapestry No.66. Ink-drawn Guardian Dog with Bared Teeth. In the early fifteenth century Manichaeanism had become increasingly under attack. The growing ferocity of the guardian dogs may reflect the community's growing sense of vulnerability. Courtesy Kanko Boko Preservation Association.

10.4

Detail of Ink-Painted Tapestry No.79. Pairs of Light and Dark guardian dogs with triple Curly Grass tails are shown on a Light and Dark striped ground. Courtesy Kankoboko Preservation Association.

10.5

Detail of Ink-Painted Tapestry No.79. Triple scroll motif. Courtesy Kanko Boko Preservation Association.

10.6

Close-up detail of a weft-faced tapestry weave with single dovetailing joins. After Irene Emery, The Primary Structures of Fabrics: An Illustrated Classification (New York: Spiral Press, 1966), 80, fig. 96.

10.4

After the main topics were woven in, the outlines and details were added using black ink and a pen, drawing directly on the wool surface. Outlining and detailing with black ink has been a feature of Uyghur painting since at least the eighth century. The ink drawings appear on only one side of the tapestries. Similar topics are drawn on some tapestries but there are no two ink-painted tapestries that are identical. Paper cartoons may have facilitated the replication of a general outline for some of the popular forms. These include the many peacock, crane and peony images.

Irene Emery describes the insertion of eccentric wefts as follows: 'The non-horizontal use of wefts for outlining and the possibility of weaving wedges and other inserts suggest that part of the unusual flexibility of tapestry weave is due to its relative freedom from a rigidly rectangular relationship between warp and weft and to the ease with which the density of the wefts can be controlled and varied without varying the weft-faced quality of the weave. One of the most notable results to be achieved by manipulation of weft density is the creation of truly curvilinear figures, not just the

126

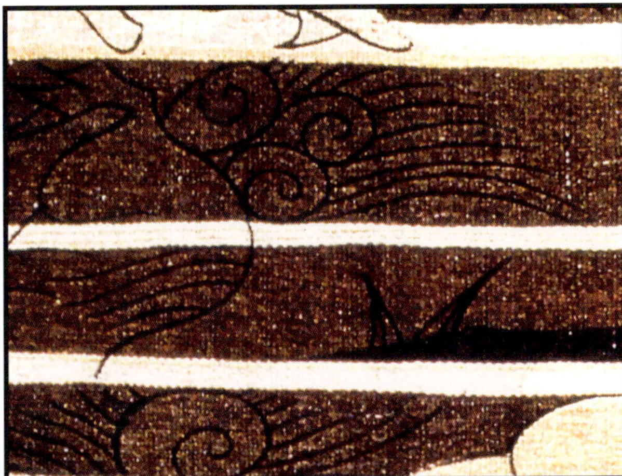

10.5

10.6

10.7

curved effects that are produced, in strictly rectangular interlacings, by fine gradations of the density and compass of the weft. In successive passages a weft being used to form a curved figure deviates more and more from the normal horizontal to follow the developing contour'.[135]

The choice of tapestry technique with inserts of eccentric wefts well reflects the aesthetic preferences of the Uyghur Manichaeans, their dedication to curvilinear forms, rejection of right angles and rectangular shapes, and their apparent delight in the unexpected and irregular.

COLOURS

Weft colours are dark red, pink, light green, light indigo, light yellow, dark brown, light brown and white. Natural colours of the wool – dark and light-brown hues, white – were used undyed. The warps of the safflower-red background stripes have now oxidised to various shades of brown and beige on the oldest examples.

SIZE

Most of the Kyoto painted tapestries average around 1.75 metres in length by approximately 1.2 metres in width. Wear

10.7

Ink-Painted Tapestry No.76 shows the peacock, five cranes, the peony and apricot blossoms. The Curly Grass motifs and a fungus appear on the background of Light and Dark segments. The White Tiger guards below. The background shade of safflower red is interrupted by swathes of dark indigo and off-white. Ink-drawn Curly Grass motifs, swirls, and spirals appear. Warp: 9 warps per per 2.5 cm. Weft: 36 wefts per 2.5 cm. 175 x 109 cm. Courtesy Kankoboko Preservation Association.

10.9

10.10

10.8 (*previous page*) *Detail of Ink-Painted Tapestry No.62. Peonies and a fungus surround a painting of a fragmented peacock. Courtesy Tsuki Boko Preservation Association.*

10.9
The ink-painted tapestries are hung vertically on the Kyoto festival floats, as well as in exhibitions in the Associations' meeting houses. Ink-Painted Tapestry No.68 in its red rasha frame is being hung for a photography session at the Kyoto Cultural Property Exhibition Room at Sakura Bank, Kyoto in 1994.

10.10
Detail of Fig. 9.19, Ink-Painted Tapestry No.84. The doves' bodies alternate between Dark and Light as do the paired guardian dogs in the centre circle. Ovoid forms may suggest Light swallowing Dark. The tails of all the guardian dogs in this example are composed of three Curly Grass motifs. Courtesy Houka Boko Preservation Association.

130

and tear have caused variations, but these seem to be the approximate original target dimensions of the weavers. They vary in size because they were woven by individual artisans creating custom weavings for diverse clients. Three of the surviving examples are much smaller in width than the others. It may be hypothesised that they were woven for the use of young acolytes.

DATING

In 1994 a thread from Ink-Painted Tapestry No.69 was radio-carbon (C-14) dated to 1398–1527 CE with 95% probability.[136]

BORDERS

Many of the ink-painted tapestries are bordered on two sides by a set of narrow multi-coloured stripes or a running fret (missing intermittently on some examples). The function of the coloured stripes is reportedly to facilitate visualisation.

Between the stripes the fields are filled with tapestry-woven and ink-drawn designs showing a dense jumble of soaring birds, vigilant beasts or marine life. The safflower red backgrounds are interrupted by swathes of dark indigo and off-white,

10.11

10.12

all covered with ink-drawn 'curly grass'
motifs framed by multiple swirls and
spirals. Some individual motifs are hard to
distinguish today because they were drawn
in black on grounds that have oxidised to a
deep brown. In addition, where identifiable,
motifs are often partial, or deliberately
splintered. The use of fractured images
is in keeping with the distortion in
perspective seen in early fifteenth-century
Manichaean miniatures uncovered in
western China. An Uyghur Manichaean
book illustration with distorted images is
depicted by Esin.[137]

FRAMING

The ink-painted tapestries have all been
uniformly framed in Kyoto with bright
red imported wool fabric, *rasha*, which was
woven in England and exported to Japan
during the Edo period (1600–1868),
continuing through the Meiji period
(1868–1912). The imported border fabric
serves to accentuate the otherworldliness
of the hangings. In Japan of this period
both the red colour and the fuzzy wool
texture were perceived as exotic. The red
rasha frames were also a means of enlivening
tapestries whose dyes had become faded

10.13

10.13

132

An untailored garment called a 'crane mantle' (jiangyi) by the Chinese scholars who excavated it, from the tomb of the Taoist Yan Deyuan. On this Taoist garment the cranes are placed along the border. On the mantles worn by the Manichaean priesthood, the crane motifs appear on the centre field. This mantle was discovered in a tomb near Datong, Shanxi province, Jin Dynasty, 1189/90 CE. Embroidered silk, 234 x 135 cm [142]. *After Verity Wilson, 'Cosmic Rainment: Daoist Traditions of Liturgical Clothing in Chinese and Central Asian Textiles', in* Selected articles from Orientations 1983-1997: *143.*

over the centuries. The red borders helped to preserve uniformity in the festival procession. The Associations wished to create and maintain harmony as a goal of the festival.

FORMAT AND FUNCTION

For a long time the layouts of the tapestries' designs were as baffling as their significance. In Kyoto the weavings have been displayed vertically for centuries, a presentation that has obscured their function. After much examination, and the use of paper models turned this way and that,[138] it was determined that the ink-painted tapestries were intended to be viewed horizontally.[139]

Their design layout and size suggest a rectangular cloth meant to wrap the human body. When an ink-painted tapestry is worn as a mantle, draped over the shoulders, the main motif appears at centre back of the upper body. Secondary motifs appear on either side above and below the main motif, front and back. These motifs show on the shoulders and hips when the garment is worn.

In 2010 I met with Prof. Lin Lecheng, Director of the Fibre Arts Institute,

Academy of Arts and Design, Tsinghua University, at his offices and studio in Beijing. Several colleagues had suggested his name as a Chinese scholar who had earnestly studied the ink-painted tapestries and their designs. Prof. Lin was able to confirm that the ink-painted tapestries were indeed designed as costumes. They were worn as mantles in northwest China and possibly in southern China's coastal communities as well.

It seems that religious functionaries have frequently worn some form of a mantle, sometimes over tailored robes. Shamans in northwest China wore a mantle adorned with 'magic' Shamanistic symbols.[140] Buddhist priests in Japan traditionally wore a patchwork mantle called a *kesa*, often of silk brocades fitted together in a meaningful scheme, the number of patches determined by the status of the priest. It is meant to emulate the patchwork mantle of rags said to have been worn by the historic Buddha. Mantles called 'Robes of Descent' were worn by Taoist priests [10.13]. A mantle worn as a costume element, in similar fashion to the practice of Manichaean *electi*, appears on the unrelated mantles of the Chilkat of northwest Canada and southeast Alaska [10.11].[141]

NOTES

133. See Ink-painted tapestries Nos. 60, 61.

134. Technical information was generously supplied by conservators Vera Indenbaum and Yadin Larochette, and weaver Mary Jane Leland.

135. Irene Emery, *The Primary Structures of Fabrics: An Illustrated Classification* (Washington, D.C. The Textile Museum, 1966), Figs. 95, 96, 108.

136. Research Laboratory for Archaeology and the History of Art at the University of Oxford, *Report on Radiocarbon Dating by Accelerator Mass Spectrometry*, 1995.

137. Emel Esin, *Antedcedents and Development of Buddhist and Manichaean Art in Eastern Turkestan and Kansu.* Pl. XXXIV, Fig. 2. See floating blossoms and outlining in sepia and black.

138. Yo-ichiro Hakomori, Professor of Architecture, University of Southern California, confirmed this determination (personal communication).

139. Lin Lecheng, Professor of Design, Tsinghua University, Beijing, explained that the function of the ink-painted tapestries was costume intended to drape the human body (personal conference in his studio, Beijing October 15, 2007).

140. Schram, *The Monguors*, vol. 2, 83.

141. Cheryl Samuel, *The Chilkat Dancing Blanket* Seattle, WA: Pacific Search Press, 1982, 31.

142. After Verity Wilson, 'Cosmic Raiment: Daoist Traditions of Liturgical Clothing,' *Orientations* 26, No.5, May 1995, 42–49, after *Wenwu* 1978:4, pl. 2:3.

11

PAINTED TAPESTRIES ON CHINA'S SOUTHERN COAST

My research trips to China were not made in an orderly consecutive geographic fashion. I was searching for clues and I returned to some cities twice, notably Lanzhou, the capital of Gansu and site of the Lanzhou Provincial Museum, where a small collection of ink-painted tapestries is preserved. In 2005 I visited the southeast coast and met there with the late Prof. Gao Hanyu who discussed with me the history of the ink-painted tapestries in the region.

During the Southern Song Dynasty (1127–1278 CE) it was illegal for a Uyghur priest to settle in China proper, and the teaching of Manichaeanism was forbidden. Earlier, Uyghur Manichaeans and their descendants had been tolerated because the Tang government (618–906 CE) relied on their substantial military support.

During the Ming Dynasty laws were enacted making the practice of Manichaean religion illegal. Taoist practices, more acceptable to the Ming rulers, were promoted. Many Manichaean houses of worship survived disguised as Taoist temples.[143]

Life in northwest China became increasingly challenging for Manichaean

11.1

Ink-painted tapestry. Images of Mount Horai, mythical home of the Taoist Immortals, are filled with chrysanthemum blossoms, symbolising long life. The islands are surrounded by flying cranes, believed to be mounts of the Immortals. The crane is also a symbol of longevity, an attribute of Sei Obo, a Taoist spirit whose palace was in the mountains where the Peaches of Immortality grow. Circa nineteenth century. 171 x 130 cm. Private collection.

11.2

11.3

136

11.2

Map of southern coastal China. by J.C.B. Mohr (Paul Siebeck), Tubingen, xxii, 2.edition, revised and expanded by Dr David Wu. From Lieu, 1992.

11.3

Prof. Zhang pointed out that Liao Dynasty flower sprays (Fig. 11.4) reappear embroidered or brocaded on the late-nineteenth-century gowns worn by female courtiers of Cixi, last Empress of China.

believers. They began to flee south, following charismatic religious leaders. The refugees were led by a dedicated cleric (a *Hu-lu fa-shih*) to sites along the Chinese coast.[144]

Once there, the migrant Uyghur Manichaean weavers and painters attempted to establish workshops to produce the ink-painted tapestries they and their ancestors had formerly created to serve as garments for the priesthood. In the southern coastal sites they could no longer easily obtain the superior-quality Gansu-Qinghai wool. Instead they used the crimpy wool sheared from the local marshland sheep. This wool

has frequently been misidentified as 'goat hair'. It is fairly stiff, coarse, and relatively thin, and is produced by 'marshland sheep' which of necessity graze in the swampy terrain of southern coastal China.[145]

In Nanjing in 1998, I had the opportunity to interview an elderly weaver named Tao Ying He. Although he was in his seventies he was proud to have been employed as a professional dyer for over forty years at the No.2 Nanjing Weaving Factory. According to Jin Wen, then director of the Nanjing 'Yunjin' Silk Fabrics Research Institute, Uyghur dyers

11.4

and weavers first settled in Nanjing during the Yuan period.

Jin Wen, himself a noted weaver, described two sites where British commercial firms had established wool-weaving workshops producing ink-painted tapestries for sale to tourists. These factories, seemingly established by the eighteenth century, were using local Chinese wool. One firm was located in Tangyang town, Dongtai county, Jiangsu province. The other was located in Longdu town, Jiangning county, Jiangsu province. Tao Ying He and Prof. Jin Wen agreed

that the ink-painted tapestries, which Tao Ying He called *Nanjing Mao Fan Jya*, were still being offered for sale during the 1970s at the curiosity shops that ring the Confucian Temple in Nanjing city. Tao Ying He described the weavings as being filled with images of birds and plants. He told of seeing them even earlier, in the 1940s, being used in 'foreigner's homes', and of his shock at seeing such precious objects placed on the floors of these homes.[146]

Samuel N.C. Lieu has described Uyghur Manichaean communities in Zhejiang province, in the town of Ssu-

11.4

Liao Tomb Mural. Prof. Zhang Pengchuan has pointed out the similarity in style between the sprays of flowers depicted on the Liao Dynasty (907–1125 CE) tomb walls, said to be realistic depictions of house decorations at the time, and those portrayed on the later ink-painted tapestries, such as the vases with floral sprays in Fig. 11.7.[155]

138

11.5

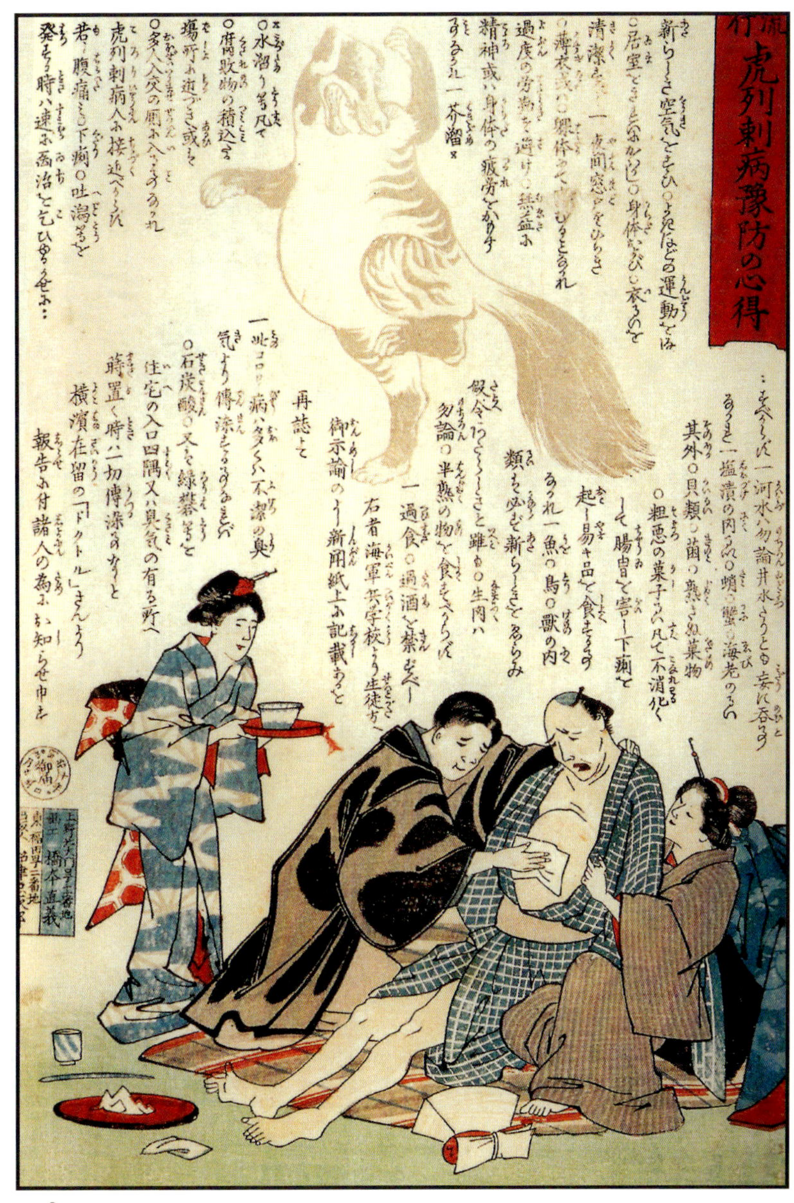

11.6

139

ming near modern Ningbo, and another
in T'ai prefecture, not far from Ningbo.
Prof. Lieu and other scholars have also
described the Cao'an Temple at the foot
of Huabiao mountain in Jinjiang county,
Fujian province, first built during the
Song dynasty (960–1279).[147] The Cao'an
shrine was finally identified with an
extant Buddhist temple annex building by
Quanzhou archaeologist Wu Wenliang in
1940. The Cao'an Temple, thought to have
served originally as a Manichaean structure,
has since become a well-publicised
archaeological site.

TS SHO 'SUZHOU' RUGS

The wife of Tse Rong Jya, the mandala
painter working in Nianduhu near
Tongren, recognised the ink-painted
tapestries, which she called *Ts sho* (perhaps
a phonetic rendering of Suzhou?). She
declared that she had seen them often
in her natal home in the city of Suzhou,
Jiangsu province. Her maternal family
presently resides in Xining City, Qinghai
province. She told of Monguor families
fleeing from the coastal towns of Nanjing
and Suzhou inland to Qinghai province in
the early Ming dynasty.

11.6
*Woodblock print, How
to Prevent Infectious
Cholera, by Hashimoto
Naoyoshi, September 1877,
published by Funatsu Chujiro.
35 x 24 cm. After Itô, Kyôko.
'Disease Prevention Prints.'
Daruma 10, No.4, Autumn
(2003): 13–27..*

11.7

11.8

11.9

Over the course of time, the Manichaean motifs appearing on the southern coastal painted tapestries were almost entirely altered to portray Taoist themes, of special significance to the surrounding Chinese neighbours. The bright red-orange safflower (Chinese *hong hua*) dye, cultivated in the northern regions of Gansu province, and traditionally used to dye the backgrounds of the tapestries, was increasingly scarce and expensive in the southern coastal regions. The safflower red-orange coloured wool was gradually

11.7
Ink-painted tapestry, five cranes motif. c. 1750–1800 CE. 178 x 127 cm. Ink-painted tapestry with wide and narrow stripes and five cranes. On this tapestry the slightly ominous cranes with their very sharp scissor-like beaks may have been a means of incorporating the protective role of the former peacock. Private collection.

11.8
Detail, end stripes of Ink-painted tapestry shown in Fig. 11.9.

11.9
Ink-painted tapestry, Jiangsu Province. The layout of the five cranes indicates this tapestry, although of fairly heavy weight and of lengthy size, was designed to be worn as costume, wrapped around the body, the largest crane placed at the centre of the wearer's back. 337 x 118 cm. Warps: cotton S-spun 4 yarns Z-plied; Wefts: wool mixed with some fragile sharp fibres, Z-spun, 2 yarns, S-plied. Private collection.

141

142

11.10

II.II

II.IO

Ink-painted tapestry, woodblock-printed design. Hand-painting eventually gave away totally to woodblock-printing. The Light and Dark stripes at the ends are retained but these are undyed natural wool colours. The square frets in the four corners enclose popular Taoist motifs including flower vases, bouquets and floral sprays. 202 x 142 cm.

II.II

Ink-painted tapestry woven in Jiangsu Province (and detail overleaf), China. C. 1750. This example of southern coastal weavings retains the prized safflower red-coloured background. The peacock motif has been reinterpreted as a stylised crane, reflecting the fading of Manichaean ideas and the ascendance of Taoist themes. The crane, said to live 1,000 years, symbolises the Taoist goal of immortality. Cranes also serve the Taoist hermit sages as conveyances across the heavens. 172 x 128 cm. Private collection.

replaced with undyed natural wool colours of grey, brown or white. The multicoloured stripes on both ends of the tapestries, though diminished in size, continued to be woven in throughout the eighteenth century and later.

The fine hand-painting of images on the tapestries became diminished and limited to the features of the crane, the Taoist symbol that replaced the Manichaean peacock on these later artworks. Interestingly, although most hand-painting disappeared, the eye of the crane, possibly continuing to reference the blessings of the deity Avalokitesvara,

continued to be painted in by hand. The Monguor descendants of the Uyghurs continued to revere Avalokitesˊvara, protector of sight. The hand painting of the eyes persisted well into the twentieth century. The other pictorial elements on these later ink-painted tapestries were produced by means of wood-block printing. Two Chinese terms used to describe this wood-block technique have been suggested. One term, provided by Prof. Zhang Pengchuan of School of Arts, Suzhou University, is *Diao Ban Yin Shua*. Another term suggested for the block-printing technique is *Chia-yen*.[148]

146

11.12

11.13

An American traveller and folk art enthusiast in the early twentieth century, Hanna Woidt, wrote about the ink-painted tapestries she encountered in the town of Suzhou.[149] The type she dubbed 'Suzhou rugs' was also produced in the town of Ningbo, as well as in the outskirts of the cities of Nanjing and Shanghai. The late Prof. Gao Hanyu, during our meeting in 2005, described the role played by western missionaries. Evidently the missionaries collected the ink-painted tapestries from weavers and dyers and brought them to art and antiques dealers in the southern coastal cities where they could be marketed.[150] The tapestries produced in Ningbo and Suzhou show motifs that reflect the taste of the potential clients for these weavings, who were now often tourists. Tropical foliage with romanticised Chinese cityscapes was frequently the topics of choice.

For their makers, including designers, dyers and weavers, these were visions of the Buddhists' Pure Land [11.12, 11.13, 11.14]. According to the Buddhist sutras, deities including the Buddhas, bodhisattvas and a few other faultless beings, inhabit a specific paradise or Pure Land, a perfect paradise,

11.12

Ink-painted tapestry depicting the town of Suzhou. The crane emblem survives with a lone image at the top. Originally designed as mantles worn as costume, the tapestries began to be designed to be viewed vertically and were marketed to tourists who used them as wall hangings or floor carpets. 160 x 120 cm. Private collection.

11.13

Detail, Fig 11.12. The crane emblem survives with a lone image at the top of this tapestry.

148

II.14

11.15

11.16

believed to be located somewhere south of India. Buddhist devotees can experience these Pure Lands during visualisation sessions and in their dreams, moving closer to Enlightenment as they focus.[151]

MERRYMAKING AND MEDICINE

Japanese antiques dealers as well as private Japanese buyers had been acquiring the ink-painted tapestries produced in the southern workshops since the Edo Period (1600–1868 CE). The weavings were sold in Kyoto and Edo (Tokyo). The southern coastal ink-painted tapestries were used as tea ceremony seating, picnic blankets and floor cloths for sake parties. The red wool cloths commonly used for festive seating are recorded in several Edo-period screen paintings and appear in Meiji period wood-block prints [11.6].

In addition to their use as party seating, the cloths were perceived to have therapeutic benefits. The safflower dye used to colour the cloths was believed in both Japan and China to have substantial medicinal properties. Safflower red is regarded as the colour of wellbeing in Japan. Even lying or resting on a safflower

11.14
Ink-painted tapestry depicting the port of Suzhou, its many gardens and canals. Being water-resistant, the ink-painted tapestries were often used as canopies on Yangtze riverboats. 160 x 120 cm. Private collection.

149

11.15
Detail of Suzhou tapestry in Fig. 11.14. Although this image of a riverboat does not show an ink-painted tapestry, they were often used as water-resistant covers on the canopies of the boats that plied the waters of the Yangtze River. Private collection.

11.16
Detail of ink-painted tapestry in Fig. 11.17. The surroundings and the architecture suggest The Pure Land. Private collection.

11.17

11.17

Ink-painted tapestry from Suzhou, providing a vista of The Pure Land, nineteenth century. Block printed with some hand-painting on the hair buns of the maidens. The stripes at the ends are becoming minimal. 160 x 120 cm. Private collection.

red textile was thought to be helpful in the restoration of good health and physical fitness. The safflower plant has actually been used in Asia to treat a variety of ailments including serious diseases such as cholera and smallpox. To the present day safflower is ingested to mitigate stomach distress.[152] In a Meiji-period woodblock print, a patient is portrayed resting on a dark-and-light-striped safflower red ink-painted tapestry of a type probably woven in a southern Chinese coastal city, as he receives the ministrations of his family and an attending doctor.

The multicoloured stripes in [11.8] were originally symbolic closures, brought together as the tapestry was wrapped around the wearer's body. The wider group of stripes would show on the outside; the narrower group would be the first wrapped and would end up closest to the body. The five colours of the stripes are red, blue, green, black and white. These colours are said by local people to represent the elements of nature: the sky, the clouds, the rivers and the earth and sun.

Prof. Zhang has offered another explanation of the multicoloured stripes consistently placed at both ends of the ink-painted tapestries. He notes that the stripes often placed above the head of the Buddha and other deities in paintings – usually described as the aureole or the many-hued rays – are also reflected in the striped borders at each end of the ink-painted tapestries.[153]

We have previously noted the extensive early collection of the Gion Festival Associations' ink-painted tapestries in Kyoto; those preserved at the Tohoku Fukushi University's Serizawa Keisuke Art and Craft Museum in Sendai, Japan; and the collection in Ōtsu, Japan. With those exceptions and a few preserved in private Japanese collections, ink-painted tapestries are in the main represented by occasional examples in a number of European and American museums, including the impressive collection preserved in the Honolulu Academy of Arts with some examples that date from the Ming dynasty.[154]

NOTES

143. Samuel N.C. Lieu, *Manichaeanism in the Later Roman Empire and Medieval China.* 2nd Edition, rev. 1992: 293–94

144. Lieu 1992: 264.

145. Personal communication Prof. Gao Hansu, vice director, Shanghai Textile Research Institute, Donghua University, Fudan University, Shanghai, August 1, 1998,

146. Personal communication, Tao Ying He, Nanjing, 1998.

147. Lieu 1992

148. Yu-Kuan Lee, *Art Rugs from Silk Route and Great Wall Areas,* (Tokyo: Oriental House Limited, 1980): 131.

149. Hannah Woidt, *Chinese Handicrafts: A Picture Book,* (Peiyang Press, Beijing 1944).

150. Personal communication, Prof. Gao Hanyu, Shanghai, PRC, 2005; Yu-Kuan Lee, *Art Rugs from the Silk Route and Great Wall Areas.*

151. Meher McArthur, *Reading Buddhist Art,* (Thames & Hudson, New York 2002): 173.

152. Takashi Hamada, M.D. Dr. Hamada is a physician and surgeon in Mie Prefecture, Japan. Personal communication, Los Angeles, August 11, 2013.

153. Personal comunication, Prof. Zhang Pengchuan, Suzhou University, November 5, 2005.

154. Accession No. 2.759. Ink-painted tapestries may also be found in the collections of the Victoria and Albert Museum, London; the Royal Ontario Museum, Toronto; the Textile Museum, Washington D.C. (Accession Nos. 1967.11.1, 1969.55.1, 1973.19.4, 1987.1.2.); the Metropolitan Museum of Art, New York; the Santa Barbara Museum of Art, California (Accession No. 76.56.4); the Museum of International Folk Art, Santa Fe, New Mexico; and the Museum of Mankind, San Diego, California.

155. Personal comunication, Prof. Zhang Pengchuan, Suzhou University, . November 5, 2005.

12 CONCLUSIONS

The mysterious origin of the textiles stored in Kyoto for over 400 years can now be identified as that portion of the Eastern Silk Route that lies in northwest China. My research took place in the years 1995 to 2010 during multiple visits to Japan and China. The textiles themselves were the primary source of information.

1. FIBRE

The textiles are wool. The Korean provenance cited by the owners was disputed as there was no production of, and little interest in, wool textiles in Korea during the thirteenth to eighteenth centuries – the period when all thirty-six wool ink-painted tapestries as well as the twenty-one wool pile audience carpets were created. A few wool ink-painted tapestries may have been transported and deposited by Uyghur forces accompanying the Mongol invaders of Korea in 1231 to 1270.

2. WOOL TYPE

The hairy wool used by the weavers of the textiles and the makers of the related audience carpets is a type characteristic of sheep raised in Gansu and Qinghai provinces, northwest China.

12.1
Detail of Fig. 11.12. Ink-painted tapestry depicting the town of Suzhou. Private collection.

3. DYES

The background design of almost all the tapestries consists of horizontal colour blocks of 'dark hues' (originally red/orange but now various shades of brown) alternating with segments of off-white. The red/orange hue is produced with safflower dye. Safflower was cultivated in northern Gansu province.

4. DESIGNS AND MOTIFS

Costume is often the repository of motifs discarded in other forms. Therefore the costumes of the nearly sixty Chinese minorities were studied. One minority, the Monguor, repeatedly used the unusual motifs seen on the ink-painted tapestries and on the audience carpets. These motifs can be seen on their dress as well as painted and carved on their surviving temples in northwest China. Texts by Von Gabain and Klimkeit have identified these motifs as Manichaean. The Uyghur 'curly grass' motif recurs on several tapestries. The peacock, a Manichaean image bestowing protection from danger, is also ubiquitous on these artworks. The consistent background design of juxtaposed segments of light and dark express the duality that is core to the Manichaean creed. On the textiles produced after the fifteenth century, Taoist motifs increasingly appear, gradually replacing the Manichaean images.

5. TECHNIQUES

The textiles are tapestry-woven and ink-painted. The people who are renowned for their special skill in combining tapestry weaving and ink-painting are the Uyghurs.

6. MAKERS

Although Uyghur peoples have been identified with the Xinjiang region, where they moved and converted to Islam in the tenth century, the Uyghur tribes who were intent on maintaining their earlier Manichaean beliefs split off and migrated eastward. They established communities along the Yellow River corridor. In time the surrounding Tibetan host population encouraged them to adopt Tibetan Buddhism, which they practise to the present day.

7. FUNCTION

The tapestries were worn as sacerdotal vestments, probably as mantles by the priestly class, 'the elect' in Manichaeanism. Their design indicates that when the tapestries are wrapped around the shoulders and hang downward, the main motifs appear at the centre back of the wearer's body, with minor motifs appearing at the shoulders and the hips.

8. EXPORT

The Monguor regularly shipped their goods along the Yellow River by raft, cargo animal or boat, to ports on the Pacific, including Tianjin, during the centuries when the textiles were exported.[156] From there, Japanese or Korean merchant ships as well as illicit Chinese vessels and multinational pirate boats probably conveyed them to Japan. [157]

9. PRODUCTION

The ink-painted tapestries may have been created in and around Zhang Jya Chuan, Tianshui district, Gansu province. After the Cultural Revolution, a few examples were discovered by museum workers in the storage vaults of the main temple in the nearby town of Qin'an, a lively commercial centre, where they were said to have been marketed. The Tianshui region's workshops were famed for producing both silk and wool tapestry for many centuries. They were originally established in the ninth century in Qinzhou, which is not far from Qin'an, and have apparently endured in some form to the present day as sites of wool tapestry and carpet production. One extant Qinzhou atelier retains a mural of a large peacock over its doorway. The peacock is the talismanic bird revered by Manichaeans and a main motif on several of the Kyoto ink-painted tapestries.

10. SPLINTER PRODUCTION

A splinter production of the ink-painted tapestries was established in southern coastal cities of Nanjing, Suzhou, and Ningbo, by refugee Monguor and Uyghur artisans from the northwest. This migration began as early as the Song dynasty and extended through the time of the Ming and Qing dynasties and the Chinese republic. The technique used to create these southern coastal tapestries is identical to that of the earlier tapestries produced in Gansu province. The tapestries are different because the wool fibre is quite distinct. The weavers of the southern coastal tapestries could no longer easily obtain the superior wool of Gansu province and were forced to use the comparatively coarse wool produced by local marshland sheep. The Taoist crane, symbol of longevity, replaced the peacock as the main motif. These coarser ink-painted tapestries nevertheless became popular with tourists and with boatmen on the Yangtze River, who used the water-repellent tapestries to protect and decorate their boat canopies.

11. THE AUDIENCE CARPETS

The twenty-one wool pile audience carpets in the collections in Japan were created in the same region by Monguors to furnish the rites led by the Tibeto-Mongol high lamas known as Living Buddhas.

In Kyoto, the dedicated members of the Gion Festival Float Associations continue to protect these rare surviving artefacts of a once-widespread philosophy, maintain the records, and display the artworks annually for the pleasure and edification of the viewing public, although in recent years replicas have replaced some originals deemed too fragile to be exposed to the elements.

156. Louis M.J. Schram, *The Monguors*, 1954, Part I: 19.
157. Marius B. Jansen, *China in the Tokugawa World*, 1992: 2–3, 5.

13
WUTUN PAINTINGS

John E. Hatherley

Although the paintings at Upper Wutun Monastery shown in Chapters 7 and 9 appear in a Monguor temple and the Monguor were once Manichaean, by the time these were painted the populace thought of themselves as Tibetan Buddhists and they were painted to honour Tibetan Buddhist deities.

MURAL PAINTINGS OF MEDITATIONAL DEITIES AT UPPER WUTUN MONASTERY
Rebkong (Tibetan)/Tongren (Chinese) is a small city in the traditional Tibetan area of Amdo, the area of northwest China that encompasses part of the provinces of Qinghai and Gansu. Five villages near Rebkong are often referred to today collectively as 'Wutun'.[158] Since the art of Wutun is generally referred to as Rebkong art, I will use the name Rebkong for both the city of Rebkong and the five villages known as Wutun.

Rebkong is known widely as a centre for what is generally described as the Rebkong school of Tibetan Buddhist art. Other than in tourist brochures, on Tibetan art websites, and excepting references in guide books, surprisingly little has been

Mural, Upper Wutun Temple. In the Mahabharata, Dhritarashtra is the King of Hastinapur at the time of the Kurukshetra War, the epic's climactic event. He was born the son of Vichitravirya's first wife, Ambika, and was fathered by Ved Vyas.

158

13.2

13.3

written about the subject. For example, there is no mention of Rebkong art in Marylin Rhie and Robert Thurman's extensive *Worlds of Transformation* or in their *Wisdom and Compassion*.[159] This essay and the descriptions it contains of examples of *tangkas* and murals do not remedy this deficiency but, hopefully, will indicate that Rebkong pictorial art and the Buddhist art of the Amdo region are fascinating subjects that warrant further detailed study. In addition to the *tangkas* and murals, Rebkong art includes sculpture, which is not discussed here.

The Rebkong area, like Amdo generally, is ethnically mixed with a long history of periodic migrations. Reflecting this, different Wutun villages have varying versions of their origins. This diversity of ideas is reflected in the culture of the area as well as in its art. According to the Scottish-born scholar and translator Gyurme Dorje, 'the Rebkhong school of art … was established by the fifteenth century and by the eighteenth century … spread to cover much of Amdo, as indeed it does today… The style broadly follows that of Central Tibet, but the infusion of cultures

13.2
Dorje Legpa, the great Buddhist Worldly Protector, riding a goat. Nyentog Monastery in Wutun, Rebkong, Amdo.

13.3
Mural, Upper Wutun Temple. Portrait of Shakyamuni, the historical Buddha, in the teaching mudra. Groups of disciples appear on either side, straining toward the Buddha in order to fully absorb his lesson.

160

13.4

13.5

generated by contact with the Mongolians, Monguor, and neighbouring Chinese, makes the work distinctive.'[160] Andreas Gruschke, a German photographer, geographer and Tibet researcher, notes that according to 'preliminary investigations', Rebkong art 'emerged in the fourteenth century when both the Sakyapa and Nyingmapa orders of Tibetan Buddhism were represented in Amdo'.[161]

Murals located in Nyenthog Monastery, some examples of which are found in this essay, provide a fascinating introduction to some of these influences. Nyanthog village

is traditionally ethnically Mongour. Today Nyenthog Monastery is Gelugpa sect, but its art reflects various sectarian influences. According to the Himalayan Art Resouces website, one side chapel includes murals 'believed to have been created during the time of Ngagchang Jamyang Lodro in the late seventeenth century. This prominent Rebkhong teacher was a student of the fifth Dalai Lama and Trichen Lodro Gyatso.'

One of the most fascinating of the surviving images is a depiction of Dorje Legpa on a mural found in one small Nyenthog chapel [13.2]. Dorje Legpa

13.4

A mural of Virudhaka.

13.5

Coffered ceiling mural in the Nyentog Monastery in Wutun, Rebkong, Amdo. The monastery is believed to have been created in the late seventeenth century, time of the prominent teacher Ngagchang Jamyang Lodro, a student of the 5th Dalai Lama and Trichen Lodro Gyatso.

13.6

162

is a worldly protector subjugated by Padmasambhava and generally associated with the Nyingma sect of Tibetan Buddhism as a guardian of Revealed Treasures or *terma*. According to Himalayan Art Resouces, this and other images in the chapel are said to be in the mixed style of the original Menri of Manla Dondrub and Khyenri and are also 'believed to have been created during the time of Ngagchang Jamyang Lodro in the late seventeenth century.'

This and other Nyenthog Monastery structures and some of the pictorial art they contain survived the Cultural Revolution through the use of chapels as storehouses. During this turbulent period some murals were additionally protected when they were covered by a thin layer of mud, which was removed when the danger of destruction abated.

13.6

This mural illustrates Vrudhaka (left) and Dhritarashtra (right), two of the four Direction Guardians (Guardian Kings). Virudhaka is the Guardian King of the South. Dhritarashtra is the Guardian King of the East and King of the celestial musicians.

NOTES

158. Andreas Gruschke, *The Cultural Monuments of Tibet's Outer Provinces: Amdo*, 2 vols. Bangkok: White Lotus, 2001.

159. Marylin M. Rhie and Robert A.F. Thurman, *Worlds of Transformation* (New York: Tibet House, 1999); Marylin M. Rhie and Robert A.F. Thurman, *Wisdom and Compassion* (New York: Abrams, 1991).

160. Dorje, Gyurme. *Footprint Tibet.* Chicago: Passport Books, 1996.

161. Gruschke, Andreas. *The Cultural Monuments of Tibet's Outer Provinces: Amdo*, 2 vols. Bangkok: White Lotus, 2001.

Acknowledgements

In China I am grateful for the insights provided by the late Prof. Gao Hanyu, Shanghai, Prof. Zhang Pengchuan, Suzhou, Prof. Chen Bingying, Lanzhou, and Prof. Lin Lecheng, Beijing. In Lanzhou Province the staff of the Gansu Provincial Museum was generous with their time and repeated efforts to assist my research. On multiple occasions they retrieved from storage the ink-painted tapestries in the museum's holdings related to those held in the Kyoto collections.

In Tianshui, China, Dr Ni Zhenmin, his wife, Prof. Wang Su, and the Ni family provided guidance and hospitality. In California, Dr Ni offered continuous insight, help and suggestions during the progress of the research. Dr David Yu provided geographic expertise and Christina Yu has been consistently helpful and supportive. I am grateful for the friendship and continuous help of Professor Kevin Stuart and for the Chinese language assistance provided by his students at Qinghai Normal University, Dr Chen Chang, Tashi Stanley and Sonan Jetsun, as well as for translating help and guidance provided by Ms Liu Xiaoyan in 2006.

In Japan I am indebted to the Japan Foundation for their early support, for the hospitality and encouragement I received at Nichibunken in 1994, for the erudition and assistance of Yoshida Kojiro, and Kajitani Nobuko. At the Osaka Museum of Ethnography, insight to the Northeast Silk Route was bestowed by Prof. Ohtsuka Kazuyoshi. Annual meetings in Tokyo with the late Prof. Yamanobe Tomoyuki as well as with textile connoisseur Morita Tadashi proved consistently enlightening. Years of help and support were provided by Kazuko Kotsugi Stearns, Dr Kuga Noriko, by Dr Nagahara Hiroyuki, and by Dr Hamada Ayumi.

Special thanks for guiding my research are due Dr Hong Cheng, Librarian, East Asian Library at UCLA. For reviewing the ideas and discussing the manuscript, my thanks to Prof. Lothar Von Falkenhausen of UCLA, Prof. Samuel Lieu of MacQuarie University, Australia, and Dr Benda Focht of the Riverside Metropolitan Museum, California. Thanks also to the Buddhist scholar John Hatherley for his contributions to this book in respect of the Wutun paintings and to Dayuan Fu, Architect, for enlightening me about the Longxing Rotating Library and its relationship to prayer cylinders.

I am grateful for the many kindnesses provided by Director Marla Berns, and my former colleagues at the Fowler Museum at UCLA, and particularly for the superb efforts of Don Cole, Museum Photographer. The entire Fowler Museum at UCLA staff were consistently supportive and generous with their advice during the preparation of this volume.

Finally my thanks to the team at Hali Publications in London, Daniel Shaffer, Liz Dixon, Ben Evans and Brian David for editing, designing, packaging and producing the book.

IMAGE CREDITS

Photographed with the permission of Gion Matsuri Yamaboko Rengokai (Gion Festival Float Associations), Kyoto. Photographs by Sei Yuge, 1991:
1.1, 2.1, 3.1, 3.4, 3.6-3.22, 3.26, 3.29, 4.3, 4.5, 5.1, 5.3, 5.4, 5.5, 6.1, 6.9, 7.1, 7.5, 7.7, 7.8, 7.10, 7.14, 7.23, 7.25, 9.1, 9.10, 9.19, 9.20-9.23, 10.1-10.8, 10.11

Calligraphy and Curly Grass motif drawing by Shuteng Feng:
3.2, 3.3

Photographed with the permission of Gion Matsuri Yamaboko Rengokai (Gion Festival Neighbourhood Float Associations), Kyoto. Photographs by the Author, 1994:
4.6, 7.15

Photographs by the Author:
4.7, 4.8, 4.9-4.11, 4.15-4.17, 4.18, 4.20, 5.2, 5.6-5.8, 6.10, 7.9, 7.11, 7.12, 7.19, 7.24, 7.25, 9.3, 9.8, 9.9, 9.11, 9.12, 9.13, 9.14, 9.24-9.36, 9.37-9.51, 10.13, 12.1

Photographs by John Hatherley:
6.3, 6.8, 7.21, 9.21

Photograph by Emily Segal:
7.16

Image ©Fowler Museum at UCLA, photographs by Don Cole:
6.4, 6.6, 9.15, 11.1-11.16

Photograph by Dr. Keith W. Slater:
9.16

Photograph by Katrin Hatherley:
9.40

Image © Staatliche Museen zu Berlin, Museum für Asiatische Kunst. Photograph by A. Papadopolous:
7.17

BIBLIOGRAPHY

AHMED, MONISHA. *Living Fabric: Weaving among the Nomads of Ladakh Himalaya.* Bangkok: Orchid, 2002.

AINSCOUGH, THOMAS M. *Notes from a Frontier.* Shanghai, China: Kelly and Walsh, 1915. Reprinted Taipei, Taiwan: Ch'eng Wen, 1971.

ASMUSSEN, JES PETER. *Manichaean Literature: Representative Texts Chiefly from Middle Persian and Parthian Writings.* Persian Heritage Series 22. Delmar, NY: Scholars' Facsimiles & Reprints, 1975.

BEDUHN, JASON DAVID. *The Manichaean Body: In Discipline and Ritual.* Baltimore, MD: Johns Hopkins University Press, 2000.

BHATTACHARYA-HAESNER, CHHAYA. *Central Asian Temple Banners in the Turfan Collection of the Museum für Indische Kunst, Berlin.* Berlin: Dietrich Reimer Verlag, 2003.

BOXER, CHARLES RALPH. *Portuguese Merchants and Missionaries in Feudal Japan, 1543–1640.* Collected Studies Series CS 232. London: Variorum Reprints, 1986.

BURKITT, F. CRAWFORD. *The Religion of the Manichees.* Donnellan Lectures for 1924. Cambridge: Cambridge University Press, 1925.

BUSSAGLI, MARIO. *Central Asian Painting.* Treasures of Asia. New York: Rizzoli, 1979.

CHEN, BINGYING. *Zhongguo shaoshu minzu ke Xue Ji Shushi Congshu* [Chinese minority peoples and the history of scientific technology]. Nanning, China: Guangxi Kexue Jishu Chubanshe, 1996.

CULTURAL CHINA. 'Beams inside the Manichaean Hall.' http://history.cultural-china.com/en/164H3736H10340.html, accessed May 7, 2013.

DE RACHEWILTZ, IGOR AND VOLKER RYBATZKI WITH COLLABORATION OF HUNG CHIN-FU. *Introduction to Altaic Philology: Turkic, Mongolian, Manchu,* Handbook of Oriental Studies, Section Eight, Central Asia, Vol 20. Brill. Leiden, The Netherlands 2010.

DENNY, JOYCE WATT, Textiles in the Mongol and Yuan Periods in *The World of Khubilai Khan: Chinese Art in the Yuan Dynasty.* New York: Metropolitan Museum of Art, 2010.

DORJE, GYURME. *Footprint Tibet.* Chicago: Passport Books, 1996.

DROMPP, MICHAEL. *Tang China and the Collapse of the Uighur Empire: A Documentary History.* Brill's Inner Asian Library 13. Leiden: Brill, 2005.

EDITORIAL COMMITTEE OF SHANGHAI THEATRICAL COLLEGE. *Ethnic Costumes and Clothing Decorations from China.* Hong Kong: Hai Feng, 1986.

EILAND, MURRAY L. *Chinese and Exotic Rugs.* Boston: New York Graphic Society, 1979.

EMERY, IRENE. *The Primary Structures of Fabrics: An Illustrated Classification.* Washington, D.C. The Textile Museum, 1966.

ESIN, EMEL. *Antecedents and Development of Buddhist and Manichaean Art in Eastern Turkistan and Kansu.* Istanbul: Milli Egitim Basimevi, 1967.

FERRAR, REGINALD. *The Rainbow Bridge.* London: E. Arnold, 1921.

FRANCK, IRENE M., AND DAVID M. BROWNSTONE. *The Silk Road: A History.* New York and Oxford, England 1986.

FUSHI, WANG AND CHEN HONGGUANG, DAI PING, DING JIASHENG, HU NANXIN, HU YUXIN, JIAN YUN, LI RUIDING, LI YOUEN, LIU YONGHUA, QIU ZHONGMING , YING YUNAN, YUAN XIAHONG, ZHANG PEICHU. *Ethnic Costumes and Clothing Decorations From China.* Hai Feng Publishing Company Ltd. Sichuan People's Publishing House.

GABAIN, ANNEMARIE. *Das Leben im uigurischen Königreich von Qočo: 850–1250.* Weisbaden, Germany: Harrassowitz, 1973.

GAUBATZ, PIPER RAE. *Beyond the Great Wall: Urban Form and Transformation on the Chinese Frontiers.* Stanford, CA: Stanford University Press, 1996.

GONICK, GLORIA GRANZ. 'Foreign Textiles at the Gion Festival.' *The Japan Foundation Newsletter* 22, No.4, 1995.

GONICK, GLORIA GRANZ. *Matsuri! Japanese Festival Arts.* Los Angeles: UCLA Fowler Museum of Cultural History, 2002.

GRUSCHKE, ANDREAS. The Cultural *Monuments of Tibet's Outer Provinces: Amdo,* 2 vols. Bangkok: White Lotus, 2001.

GULÁCSI, ZSUZSANNA. *Manichaean Art in Berlin Collections.* Corpus Fontium Manichaeorum: Series Archaeologica et Iconographica. Belgium: Brepols, 2001.

GULÁCSI, ZSUZSANNA. *Mediaeval Manichaean Book Art: A Codicological Study of Iranian and Turkic Illuminated Book Fragments from Eighth to Eleventh Century East Central Asia.* Nag Hammadi and Manichaean Studies 57. Leiden, Netherlands: Brill, 2005.

GRUSCHKE, ANDREAS. *The Cultural Monuments of Tibet's Outer Provinces: Amdo,* vol. I, *The Qinghai Part of Amdo.* Bangkok: White Lotus, 2001.

HAKOMORI, YO-ICHIRO. 'The Sacred and the Profane in *Matsuri* Structures.' In *Matsuri! Japanese Festival Arts.* Los Angeles: UCLA Fowler Museum of Cultural History, 2002.

HASLUND, HENNING, trans. Elizabeth Sprigge and Claude Napier. *Men and Gods in Mongolia.* 1935; reprint, Stelle, IL: Adventures Unlimited Press, 1992.

HOPKIRK, PETER. *Foreign Devils on the Silk Road: The Search for the Lost Cities and Treasures of Chinese Central Asia.* Amherst, Massachusetts University of Massachusetts Press 1980.

ITÔ, KYÔKO. 'Disease Prevention Prints.' *Daruma* 10, No.4, Autumn, 2003.

JANSEN, MARIUS B. *China in the Tokugawa World.* Campring, MA: Harvard University Press, 1992.

JI, GHANG LIAN. *Si lu, zou lang de bao gao: Gan Qing te you min zu wen hua xing tai yan jiu* [Researches on the Cultural Formation of the Ethnic Groups Which Live Only in Gansu and Qinghai]. Beijing: Min zu chu ban she, 1999.

KAJITANI, NOBUKO AND KOJIRO YOSHIDA. *Gion Matsuri Yamaboko Kensohin Chosa Hokokusho: Torai Senshokuhin no Bu* [Catalog of the Gion Festival float decorations: the imported hangings]. Kyoto: Gion Matsuri Yamaboko Rengokai, 1992.

KARIMOVA, USMANOVNA RISALAT. 'Uighur Rugs: The Tradition of Figural Designs.' *Ghereh: International Carpet & Textile Review* 10, No.31, 2002.

KLIMKEIT, HANS-JOACHIM. *Manichaean Art and Calligraphy.* Leiden, Netherlands: Brill, 1982.

KLIMKEIT, HANS-JOACHIM. *Gnosis on the Silk Road: Gnostic Parables, Hymns & Prayers from Central Asia.* New York: HarperCollins, 1993.

LEE, YU-KUAN. Art *Rugs from Silk Route and Great Wall Areas,* Tokyo: Oriental House Limited, 1980.

LIEU, SAMUEL N. C. *Manichaeism in the Later Roman Empire and Medieval China.* Manchester, UK: Manchester University Press, 1985.

LIEU, SAMUEL N. C. *Manichaeism in Central Asia and China.* Nag Hammadi and Manichaean Studies 45. Boston: Brill, 1998.

MCARTHUR, MEHER. *Reading Buddhist Art: An Illustrated Guide to Buddhist Signs and Symbols.* New York: Thames & Hudson, 2002.

MORIYASU, TAKAO. 'The Flourishing of Manichaeism under the West Uighur Kingdom. New Edition of the Uighur Charter on the Administration of the Manichaean Monastery in Qoco.' In *World History Reconsidered through the Silk Road.* Osaka University Twenty-First Century COE Program, Interface Humanities Research Activities 2002/2003. Osaka, Japan: Osaka University, 2003.

MORIYASU, TAKAO. *A Study on the History of Uyghur Manichaeism: Research on Some Manichaean Materials and Their Historical Background,* Memoirs of the Faculty of Letters, Osaka University 31–32. Osaka, Japan: Osaka University, 1991.

MOTOSHI, OKA. 'Local Society in Southeastern Coastal Zhejiang and Manichaeism During the Song and Yuan Periods.' Panel presentation, Interarea Session 27, Association for Asian Studies Conference, San Francisco, CA, April 6–9, 2006.

NORBU, KALSANG, ZHU YONGZHONG, AND KEVIN STUART. 'A Ritual Winter Exorcism in Gnyan Thog Village, Qinghai.' *Asian Folklore Studies* 58, 1999.

OHTSUKA, KAZUYOSHI. *Ainu Moshiri: Minzoku Mon'you kara Mita Ainu no Sekai* [The world of the Ainu through their design motifs]. Osaka, Japan: National Museum of Ethnology, 1993.

RACHEWILTZ, IGOR DE AND VOLKER RYBATZKI WITH COLLABORATION OF HUNG CHIN-FU. *Introduction to Altaic Philology: Turkic, Mongolian, Manchu,* Handbook of Oriental Studies, Section Eight, Central Asia, Vol 20 Brill. Leiden, The Netherlands 2010, 45-46, Figures 2, 3.

RHIE, MARYLIN M., AND ROBERT A. F. THURMAN. *Worlds of Transformation,* New York: Tibet House, 1999.

ROSTOV, CHARLES I. AND JIA GUANYAN, *Chinese Carpets.* New York: Harry N. Abrams, 1983.

RUNCIMAN, STEVEN. *The Medieval Manichee: A Study of the Christian Dualist Heresy.* 1947; repr., Cambridge, UK: Cambridge University Press, 1982.

RUSSELL-SMITH, LILLA. *Uygur Patronage in Dunhuang: Regional Art Centres on the Northern Silk Road in the Tenth and Eleventh Centuries.* Leiden: Brill, 2005.

SAMUEL, CHERYL. *The Chilkat Dancing Blanket*. Seattle, WA: Pacific Search Press, 1982.

SCHRAM, LOUIS M. J. *The Monguors of the Kansu–Tibetan Frontier*. 3 vols. Transactions of the American Philosophical Society. Philadelphia: American Philosophical Society, 1954–61.

SCHWARZ, HENRY. *The Minorities of Northern China A Survey*. Bellingham, WA: Western Washington University, 1984, 115.

SERIZAWA, CHOSUKE. *Ainu Bunkaten* [Exhibition of Ainu Culture]. Sendai, Japan: Tᵓohoku Fukushi Daigaku Serizawa Keisuke Bijutsu Kᵓogeikan, 1990.

SHARENKOFF, VICTOR N. *Study of Manichaeism in Bulgaria with Special Reference to the Bogomils*. New York: Carranza, 1927.

SLATER, KEITH W. *A Grammar of Mangghuer: A Mongolic Language of China's Qinghai–Gansu Sprachbund*. London: Routledge, 2003.

STEIN, R.A. *Tibetan Civilization*, Stanford: Stanford University Press, 1972.

TEKIN, TALÂT. *A Grammar of Orkhon Turkic*. Uralic and Altaic Series 69. Bloomington, IN: Indiana University Publications, 1968.

University of Oxford Research Laboratory for Archaeology and the History of Art, Unpublished Report, *Report on Radiocarbon Dating by Accelerator Mass Spectrometry*, May 5, 1995.

WANG, HAIYAN AND CHAO, SHENGLIN EDS. *Hometown of the Rainbow*. Huzhu, Qinghai, China, Government of Huzhu Tu Nationality Autonomous County, 1994.

WATT, JAMES C. Y. DENNY, JOYCE. Textiles in the Mongol and Yuan Periods in *The World of Khubilai Khan: Chinese Art in the Yuan Dynasty*. New York: Metropolitan Museum of Art, 2010.

WATT, JAMES C. Y. AND ANNE E. WARDWELL. *When Silk Was Gold: Central Asian and Chinese Textiles*. New York: Metropolitan Museum of Art, 1997.

WILSON, MING AND VERITY WILSON. ED., with the Palace Museum, Beijing. *Imperial Dress in The Qing Dynasty*. London: Victoria and Albert Museum, 2010.

WILSON, VERITY. 'Cosmic Raiment: Daoist Traditions of Liturgical Clothing.' *Orientations* 26, No.5, May 1995.

WOIDT, HANNA. *Chinese Handicrafts*. Beijing: Peiyang, 1944.

WU-SHU, LIN. *Mo ni jiao ji qi dong jian* [Manichaeism and its eastward expansion]. Taipei, Taiwan: Shu Xin, 1997.

YAN, ZHENGDE AND YIWU WANG, ED. *Qinghai Baike Dacidian* [Qinghai Encyclopedic Dictionary]. Zinghai Baike Dacidian. Beijing: China Financial and Economic Press, 1994.

YANG, FUXUE. 'Where Did the Ganzhou Uighurs Go After the Kingdom Collapsed?' *A Summary of the Research of History of Northwest Minorities, Dunhuang Studies.* The Almanac of Research of Minority History in China. Beijing: Minzu Press, 1994.

YONGZHONG, ZHU. 'Wutu.' YouTube video, 31:05. May 3, 2011, https://www.youtube.com/watch?v=IPMthBldYYo.

YOSHIDA, KOJIRO. 'The Gion Festival and Imported Draperies.' *Bulletin of International Research Center for Japanese Studies* 9, 1993.

INDEX

170

Front cover Ink-Painted Tapestry No.61 [7.1]. A pair of affronted peacocks surround the Manichaean deities, the Sun and the Moon. 167 x 122 cm. Courtesy Iwatori Boko Preservation Association.
Title page Pile Carpet No.40. [3.26] Turkic guls (tribal insignia) alternate with swastikas and a running fret. 177 x 99 cm. Courtesy Naginata Boko Preservation Association.
Contents page Ink-Painted Tapestry No.66 [5.5]. Peacock, magpie, and peony appear. Courtesy Naginata Boko Preservation Association.
Back cover Pile Carpet No.47. [3.22], c. 13th century. A pair of cooperating guardian dogs clutch a light and dark ribbon, rotating a prayer cylinder as they run. 169 x 99 cm. Courtesy Naginata Boko Preservation Association.

Early Carpets and Tapestries on the Eastern Silk Road

© Gloria Gonick 2015
World Copyright reserved
ISBN 978-1-85149-810-9
ACC Art Books Ltd.

British Library Cataloguing-in-Publication Data
A catalogue record for this book is available from the British Library

Produced and Packaged by Hali Publications Ltd., London, UK + 44 (0)20 7657 1201
Editors Daniel Shaffer, Brian David
Designer Liz Dixon, Happisburgh, Norfolk, UK. +44 (0)1692 652983
Printer EBS – Editoriale Bortolazzi, Verona, Italy
Typeface Mrs Eaves-Roman 12/15

Published by ACC Art Books Ltd, Woodbridge, Suffolk, IP12 4SD, UK
Tel +44 (0)1394 389950
Email info@antique-acc.com
Web www.antiquecollectorsclub.com